AFRO-CUBAN TALES

T0327245

Afro-Cuban Tales

Cuentos negros de Cuba

LYDIA CABRERA

Translated by
Alberto Hernández-Chiroldes
and Lauren Yoder

With an introduction by
Isabel Castellanos

University of Nebraska Press
Lincoln and London

LIBRARY OF CONGRESS CATALOGING-IN-PUBLICATION DATA
[Cuentos negros de Cuba de Cuba. English]
Afro-Cuban tales = Cuentos negros de Cuba / Lydia Cabrera ;
translated by Alberto Hernández-Chiroldes and Lauren
Yoder ; with an introduction by Isabel Castellenos.
p. cm.
In English.
ISBN 0-8032-1533-9 (cl. : alk. paper) – ISBN 0-8032-6438-0
(pbk. : alk. paper)
1. Blacks – Cuba – Folklore. 2. Tales – Cuba.
1. Title: Cuentos negros de Cuba. 11. Title.
GR121.C8C3213 2004   398.2′097291–dc22   2004048089

Contents

Introduction to the English Edition

ISABEL CASTELLANOS

On June 6, 1930, Lydia Cabrera paid her first visit to the home of Calixta Morales, better known in the Ocha Rite by her saint's name "Oddeddei." Teresa Muñoz, an old seamstress in her household who was also an ancient priestess in the religion of the orishas, took her there. That meeting left its permanent stamp on her. One might say that there, in Calixta's home on June 6, the day when the Catholic calendar celebrates the Feast of Saint Norbert and the Ocha Rite pays homage to Ochosi the hunter god, the storyteller and ethnographer Lydia Cabrera was truly born.

Many prior and subsequent events contributed to shaping her as a writer. However, that meeting with Calixta, Teresa Muñoz, and José de Calazán Herrera (another of her best informants) turned out to be decisive as we can see by reading her field notes, preserved today in the Cuban Heritage Collection at the University of Miami library. For example, in an ethnographical entry made that same day, Lydia describes the altar that Calixta prepared to regale her guardian orisha:

> At night the altar's set up already. Two wildcat skins embroidered with shells.
>
> On the ground, a large pot of rice and beans with popcorn. Two burning candles.
>
> By touching the ground and kissing the tips of their fingers, they bow to the altar. . . .
>
> The smell of guava fills the small room.

In "Bregantino Bregantín," the first tale in *Afro-Cuban Tales*, we find the following:

"Sanune touched the earth and kissed it on her fingertips. Prostrate at the men's feet, she lost consciousness. When she opened her eyes, she was surrounded by night, in a room thick with the smell of warm foliage and guavas. . . . She found herself before an altar made of two wildcat skins and two freshly cut poplar branches propped against the wall. On the ground she could see several soup tureens with their lids on, a horseshoe, two huge pots of rice, some red beans, and popcorn."

Calixta Morales's birthday altar ("trono de cumpleaños") in Havana is the same altar before which Sanune regains consciousness in "Bregantino Bregantín." Ethnology gives life to Cabrera's fictional works as much as her storytelling instinct gives distinctive character to her ethnological writings.

Lydia Cabrera was born in Havana on May 20, 1899, and was the youngest of eight children. Her father, Raimundo Cabrera Bosch, was a prominent lawyer and writer who had lived in exile in New York until the end of the Cuban War of Independence (1898). He displayed a special fondness for Lydia because she was the child of his later years. Prominent writers, politicians, and artists were frequent visitors in the Cabrera household. As a child, Lydia liked to paint and write, and since her father wanted to please her, he allowed her to publish her first article in *Cuba y America* (a magazine published by Don Raimundo) when she was fourteen. It was the first in a series of articles that she published during the course of almost three years under the name Nena en Sociedad. In this series Lydia writes articles hiding behind her pen name. In addition to recording weddings and baptisms, Lydia criticizes the government's indifference to culture and letters. These articles are not by any means conventional society pages. Although they may lack literary value, they are clearly precursors of Lydia's more mature style with which she began to compose tales in 1930.

Until she settled in Paris in 1927, she sometimes wrote for Havana publications, almost always to support and encourage some artistic project, as for example the restoration of the old Santa Clara convent. However, during that time Lydia wanted to be a painter, not a writer. That's why she moved to France, where she studied at the Ecole du Louvre and the Académie Contemporaine, whose director was Fernand Léger, studying under the famous painter Alexandra Exter. Her vacation in Havana in 1930 and that meeting with Teresa, Calixta, and Calazán changed the course of her life. That's when she began to write these short stories that were translated in 1936 and published in France with the title *Les Contes nègres de Cuba*.

Little by little, she devoted herself more to writing and less to painting. Her first book was well received by critics in France, but the Spanish edition didn't appear until 1940 in Cuba. After this initial volume, three more fictional works and many other ethnographic publications followed, including *El Monte*, one of the most significant books of twentieth-century Cuban literature.

Lydia's close relationship with her old Afro-Cuban friends opened up an unknown world for her. She was able to penetrate a magical cosmos in which the limits between natural and supernatural realms are tenuous, an environment in which deities are accessible and communicate directly (through spiritual possession) or indirectly (through divination). This is a reality in which seemingly inanimate beings (trees, stones, rocks) are filled with spiritual energy, or *aché*, a universe in which the gods, like human beings, eat, love, and fight. This experience can be explained through numerous myths, legends, or *patakís*, where animals possess human characteristics and interact with men and women, where a cotton plant can trap an envious bird, or where Ikú (death) herself could fall in love with a king's son. To summarize, in the world that kindled Cabrera's imagination, basic categories, the foundations of Western culture, are radically called into question.

In a variety of ways, Lydia incorporates this Afro-Cuban worldview into her tales. Some narratives are based directly on slightly modified patakís. In other cases, she recreates stories by adding incidents, themes, and characters. She bases other stories on old Afro-Cuban songs, and, in fact, in these the music becomes the central element of the story. Rather than being simply legends collected by an anthropologist, many of the tales are of her own creation, products of an imagination deeply permeated by Afro-Cuban thought.

Cabrera uses many linguistic devices to communicate Afro-Cuban life to her readers. One of these devices is to eliminate the conventional limits separating the semantic categories of people, animals, and things. For example, the princess Dingadingá is able first to marry an earthworm and later a bull. The masculine gender is eliminated from language in the kingdom of Cocozumba. Jicotea (the turtle) falls madly in love with Arere Marekén. The Almendares River dares to claim Soyan Dekín for itself. Encouraged by the flexibility that pervades the Afro-Cuban world, Cabrera juggles all limits and offers us a world upside down in which guinea hens can make Christopher Columbus and the king of Spain dance, little fat cooking pots are able to cook by themselves, the pope can send encyclicals to pumpkins, and officials can be defeated by the shrewdness of turtles. What is unreal becomes real, and what is real, unreal. To explain it in Cabrera's own words, it is "the reality of unreality." This narrative style is a forerunner of what will be known later in Latin American literature as "magical realism."

Another means employed by Cabrera to express the Afro-Cuban worldview is the use of ethnographic details within her stories, supported by meticulous descriptions of her characters, of practices, and of objects used in religious ceremonies. Many readers unacquainted with Afro-Cuban religions find that the abundance of these sensory details, such as colors, fragrances, flavors, and textures, creates a setting, a visual and olfactory reality that allows them to experience and enter into the narrative world created by the author.

Moreover, on many occasions the characters use expressions from the Bozal language, a creolized dialect now extinct, or in Lucumí, Congo, or Abakuá languages. Most of the time, however, the characters speak Spanish, using a rich Cuban vernacular full of colloquial expressions, at times archaic or at least sounding archaic. For example, "no daba un golpe," and "Yo no te dije que si te encontraba con otro Negro te hacia papilla?" Although Lydia seldom explicitly sets her tales in a particular time or space, language usage as well as the description of the landscape confirm without saying that the events take place in Cuba, some at an unspecified time and some during the colonial period.

In her tales as well as in her ethnographic work, Cabrera showed that although the Afro-Cuban vision is indeed African in origin, it is first and foremost Cuban. It is true that some of her characters are of African origin, but we also find many European elements that are essential ingredients of Cuban Creole culture. For example, the king of Spain came to dance in Havana in one of her tales. In another story, even the parrot lowered his voice on Good Friday, and only after Easter would the parliament open and the lottery begin. In a third, the bishop decreed that nobody should pay attention to a miraculous branch that had appeared on the wall of a rooming house. In other words, these magical events are set in a Cuban context and the characters are Cubans who live in rooming houses, play the lottery, and read the local press.

Despite reflecting local mores, these tales should not in any way be considered as simply the expression of local color. On the contrary, a delicate surrealism that transcends the frontiers of any national environment underlies these stories. In her own masterful way, Lydia Cabrera manages to recreate the Afro-Cuban cosmological worldview. Yet these writings are as well some of the most universal, and, paradoxically, some of the most distinctly Cuban contributions to Latin American literature.

Introduction to the Spanish Edition

FERNANDO ORTIZ

This is the first book written by a Havana-born woman. She began studying Afro-Cuban folklore with me years ago. Simple curiosity first led Lydia Cabrera to delve into the forests of Havana's black legends, and she found them truly delightful. She began transcribing and collecting those stories, and has gathered a large number. When she read some of these tales to literary personalities in Paris, they were enthralled by their poetic qualities. The poet Francis de Miomandre, himself a connoisseur of Latin American literature, translated some of the legends into French, and a perceptive editor published them in a collection called *Les Contes Nègres de Cuba*, now already out of print. Some of the tales had already been published in such prestigious literary reviews as *Cahiers du Sud, La Revue de Paris,* and *Les Nouvelles littéraires.* That's how it happened that the stories appeared first in French rather than in Spanish, their original language. The foreign critics' favorable reception of these tales and their excellent reputation thus precede the first Spanish edition.

Some of these critics praised the stories for the spontaneity of their poetry and their art; others, like E. Noulet, found the psychology of the tales quite distinct and unusual. He speaks of "a voracious sense of life, a very sensitive reaction to every form and language, a spirit that is both indolent and courageous, naive and mockingly humorous." Others, like Jean Cassou, concentrated on the social aspect of the stories,

Fernando Ortiz (Havana, 1881–1969) was an eminent Cuban ethnographer who was Lydia Cabrera's mentor and brother-in-law.

where he saw portrayed an oppressed race's pain and sadness.

Some of the stories originate from the turn of an African phrase that has been contaminated very little by cultural links with the white world. These particular stories retain their original African flavor and pathos. One critic said that the tales demonstrate "a deep immorality" and "lack any didactic intention." This was written in the 1940s. We do not know to whom the author refers. This was part of an ongoing debate. Other comments included the following: "The stories are unable to distinguish good from evil," and "they have an extraordinary talent for forgetting." All of these opinions surely come from the perspective of white men who prejudge blacks according to an ethic that white people have decided upon among themselves. In my opinion, it would be better to try to understand an ethic that is different and distinct rather than claim that morality is lacking in the stories. There are values in the tales that emerged from economic, social, and political circumstances that were surely different from white circumstances. Those circumstances developed in the blacks' traditional ancestral African culture and also in their new more artificial culture that evolved in the Americas. Perhaps it would be more productive to consider Africans, whose soul is reflected in these stories, in the same manner that we view the ancient Greek, Etruscan, or Roman civilizations. We could then develop a comparative approach for studying their mythology and social system.

We should not forget that these stories are the result of input from both Afro-Cuban folklore and the white translator. For the Spanish text is in reality also a translation, and a second translation at that. From the African languages (Yoruba, Ewe, or Bantu) in which the stories were created, they were translated in Cuba into the mixed colloquial language of Afro-

Cubans. The old black Cuban woman who told Lydia these stories may have heard them from her ancestors in a mixed Afro-Spanish language. From that dialect, Lydia had to translate the stories into a more intelligible form of Spanish, such as they now appear in this text. By keeping the stories' exotic content and form, the author has faithfully fulfilled her difficult task. This collection of stories opens a new chapter in Cuban folk literature.

For the most part, these Afro-Cuban tales are not religious stories, although many of their protagonists are indeed characters from the Yoruba pantheon, characters such as Obaogó, Ochún, Ochosí, etc.[1] Most of the stories can be classified as fables, like the fables of Aesop or the Afro-American stories of Uncle Remus, so popular among the children of our neighbor, the United States. The tiger, the elephant, the bull, the worm, the hare, hens, and above all the turtle. Or sometimes the pair turtle/deer, so typical of Yoruba folklore, in which the turtle, archetype of cleverness, always wins out over physical strength and stupidity.[2]

Some stories, like "Papa Turtle and Papa Tiger," probably originated in Cuba, because they display a combination of various folk elements, such as a unified plot followed by simple fables.

Other stories, like "Two Queens" and "Los Compadres," are about truly human characters. In these tales, mythology appears only marginally. In several other tales we see totemic traits; a good example would be the references to Tiger-Man, Bull-Man, and Papa-Turtle.

---

1. The name Obaogó seems to have been invented by Cabrera or her informants. Ochún is the goddess of love, sexuality, beauty, and diplomacy. She is often invoked in matters of love and money. Ochún is represented in the Catholic religion by the Virgin of Charity (La Virgen de la Caridad del Cobre).

2. The pair turtle/deer is "la pareja jicotea-venado, o tortuga-ciervo."

The distinction made by the god Ochosí between polygamy and prostitution is interesting. Ochosí, the male lover and hunter of the Yoruba cycles, describes the distinction this way: Polygamy is a situation in which a man, like Ochosí himself, has many permanent wives who are always well fed but whom he never pays. Prostitutes, on the other hand, work for a man.

"Bregantino Bregantín," a tale with an old traditional Spanish title, is a story that Freudians should pay attention to, because it expounds the social myth of the patriarch who kills all other men and male children. In the story, a clever mother saves one of her boys, who manages years later to destroy the power and domination of his father.

Another tale explains how the first men, the first black and the first white, came into being. In black folklore there are many myths of creation, but this one was new to me. The great creator, Oba-Ogo, made the first human by "blowing on his own excrement." This is not a very flattering myth for humans, however divine the excrement is! But it is not really very different from the biblical myth in which the first human being is created from mud, mud molded by Jehovah and to which he gives life by breathing on it with his divine breath. The black myth does not explain what early humans were like. It does say, however, that in spite of the sun's prohibition, one man climbed up on a beam of light and got his skin burnt when he got too close to the sun. Meanwhile, another man went to the moon and became white.

Most of these stories collected by Lydia Cabrera are of Yoruba origin, but I cannot with certainty say that the origin is always the same. In several tales, there is evidence of white cultural components. In other stories there are significant, interesting cases of cultural transmission, like the tales in which the narrator assigns the god to the position of secretary of the supreme court; or, in another case, captain of the fire department.

This book makes a valuable contribution to both black and white Cuban folklore literature, in spite of some negative opinions by critics stemming from forgivable ignorance or from ridiculous, prejudiced vanity. There are many people in Cuba who have negative attitudes, but true culture and progress means affirming rather than rejecting what is real. People who reject who they are will end up on a path of self-destruction. An old Afro-Cuban proverb puts it this way: "The goat who breaks a drum will pay for it with his own skin."[3]

3. "Chivo que rompe tambor con su pellejo paga."

AFRO-CUBAN TALES

Bregantino Bregantín

At the hottest time of a summer's day, in a year long since forgotten, there was a young maiden named Dingadingá[1] who
woke up from her siesta and went straight to her father the
king, announcing:

"Daddy-king, I want to get married!"

Now Dingadingá almost never opened her mouth. She was
timid, obedient, and well brought up, and this was the first
time in her life that she had ever dared to say what she really
wanted. The very first time. The king was fond of his daughter
because she never pestered him. He was quick to realize that
her request was reasonable, for in spite of the day's heat he
could see that his fifteen-year-old was in full blossom. He
looked her over for a moment, then answered:

"Fine. I'll start looking for a suitable husband for you right
away, and the choice will be yours, Dingadingá. Just be patient."

And so the good king, from his hammock swinging in the
cool of the banana grove, called one of his generals and ordered him to sound the trumpets (the ceremonial ones used
on special occasions) to call all the handsome young men to
the palace, to sound the trumpets so loudly that it would tear
from their sleep all those people dead to the world during siesta time. Now the queen, Dingadingá's mother, was an in-
veterate complainer. She always had to butt into everything to
try to get her way.

"What?!" she said, chomping furiously on her cud of tobacco. Then, after spitting it out, she stomped on it, as if the tobacco were the cause of all the commotion.

[1]. In the French version the name is spelled "Dindgadindgà."

"My daughter! Get married like that to just anyone, the first fellow who shows up? Never; no way I'll accept that. Has anyone ever seen the like? My daughter is destined for a man of great worth, someone who can prove his worth to us!"

"Of great worth? What kind of worth?" yawned the king. "A healthy, strong man. I say that Dingadingá needs to marry a strong fellow who packs a wallop!"

"In that case, marry her off to Ta Zandé's mule, who demolished her house with one kick!"

Now the king in his hammock was heavy with sleep, and he knew that his wife was about to turn a simple question into a long drawn-out argument, so he stretched his muscles and decisively turned his back to her, telling her to take all the steps she thought necessary and to let him sleep until the sea breeze began to stir.

"That's right. You think it's none of my business! But who carried Dingadingá for nine months, you or me? She'll have a husband worthy of us both. As if the girl were an animal, a dog in heat with no proper upbringing! And as if you and I both were not descendants of the first elephant who founded – thanks not to his strength but to his wisdom – this kingdom of Cocozumba! Our son-in-law must do us proud."

That's how she thought aloud, sitting at her window. Dingadingá's bright deer eyes watched the growing number of young, strong, elegantly naked suitors filling up the palace courtyard. Her mother had the ceremonial trumpets sound again. And all the young men were sent away with no explanation. They left as they had come, saying:

"How shameful! How demeaning!"

Then, as if inspired, the queen made the decision in the name of her husband that within the space of one day and the following night, on a date that the *babalaos*[2] would choose,

2. A *babalao* is a priest in the Yoruba or Lucumí religion in Cuba.

the suitor whose songs could make them both dance (the queen, whose knees had grown moldy, and the king, who would plug his ears with wax) would win Dingadingá's hand. And he would rule over Cocozumba. Later, the ancestors, seated around the fire (in the uncertain world of the dead and the not-yet-born), would remind them of the old funeral chant, saying:

"Bogguará arayé micho berere bei oku kué oku eron ogguá odgá oni ombaodgá omi okué."[3]

And the ancestors would come down to take their souls, all the souls of the body, forming into the same block of ice the blood of the dying and the blood of the choir that helps them die, only to die in turn.

For as the ancestors might say:

"He who enjoys life and living, death comes and takes him, even though he keeps saying: 'Don't take me yet. Let me stay. For when you die you're gone completely, gone completely. Nothing to do but accept. You've reached the end. Gone completely.'"

As soon as the royal edict was announced, there was not one single fellow in the whole country, whether he had a thin or a booming voice, a guitar, a drum, or even a gourd with

3. An okué is a funeral chant.

The original meaning of many of the African words in this book has been lost. After consulting dictionaries and native speakers of African languages, we have found very few translations for these words, probably because their original pronunciation has changed in Cuba. Nevertheless, they are chants that some Afro-Cubans sing. They attribute magical powers to them, and they know on what occasions to use each of the chants, but they do not know the exact meaning of the words. In the 1930s, when Lydia Cabrera published this book, there was an environment of antirationalism in art and literature; therefore, many fractured verbal utterances appeared in literature. So these chants were also part of a prevailing artistic modality. (author's note)

pebbles in it, who didn't believe that he was marked by luck and destined to win the hand of the king's daughter.

On the day chosen for the contest, the king and queen appeared ceremoniously upon the palace balcony at the crack of dawn and sat down facing each other on two stones without a glance at the many suitors who were standing like an army in front of the palace.

The first one to try, with a voice that shook the houses to their foundations, was a certain "get out of my way" kind of guy, as big as a church wardrobe. Although he managed to shake the palace and make the whole town vibrate, he couldn't get the slightest attention from the royal couple. Even when his huge vocal cords broke, huge like ships' cables, he was still full of sound from his head to his toes and could have gone on making noise indefinitely, but at the judge's signal, he was forced to yield his place to the next contestant.

The next suitor, acting on the advice of a ghost who appeared to him from time to time, had swallowed whole two lively mockingbirds and two blind canaries. Scarcely had he opened his mouth – forgetting that the ghost had warned him to relax and open his mouth only a crack – when the birds flew out. So he lost. But no one else was any luckier, not the accordion player who followed him, and not the singers who had come from the North, the South (from the Sponge Seas), the East, and the West.

Up on the balcony, the king and the queen looked like two stone statues. Dingadingá was getting bored and had not the slightest interest in watching what resulted from her innocent summer's day wish.

Then the earthworm (in those days he wasn't such a despicable character, no more disgusting than your average guy), the earthworm, who had by chance learned about the contest, showed up from the farthest corner of the kingdom. Squeezing his drum between the suitors, he made his way right up to the front row. To everyone's surprise, the next morning he began to play and sing:

"Sendengue kirito, sendengue zóra,
Sendengue, zóra!
Kerekete Ketínke!"

And the queen's face twitched with pleasure.

At nine in the evening, the king scratched one of his ears.

By ten o'clock, the wax in the king's ears had melted and the queen's joints had loosened. Up to then they could be seen only in profile. Now, with big smiles on their faces, they were facing their subjects.

At eleven o'clock, they came down the stairs hand in hand and walked around the drum.

At midnight, the ceremonial cry rang out:

"Kereketéntentén . . . Zoráa! . . ."

The king and the queen danced joyously in the street and then proclaimed Earthworm the winner and heir to the kingdom.

After all the congratulations, which couldn't quite hide all the disappointment and envy, the king, as soon as the family was alone, said to his future son-in-law:

"Take whatever you want. What's ours is yours. Pick out all the slaves you need."

"Thanks, my father-in-law," said the earthworm. "I don't want for anything and one servant is all I need. I already have one I know and trust – the bull!"

It's true that the bull had been serving the earthworm loyally for many years, ever since the earthworm had bought him during one of his trips when the bull was just a calf. In the house that the king had given to his children, the bull alone

5

took care of everything. He did all the cooking and the serving as well. He washed the dishes, swept, washed the clothes, and did the ironing without losing an iota of his dignity. He weeded the garden, worked in the fields, fed the chickens, led the cows to pasture, ran errands, and protected his master's fragile back. No one could have managed better. And when the earthworm thought it appropriate, the bull took his place and faithfully fulfilled the worm's conjugal duties with diligence. And in the same way, whenever a neighboring country declared war or whenever there was an uprising to squash, it was always the bull who went to fight in Earthworm's name, and always to his advantage.

That's the way it was when Earthworm, in the third year of his marriage, could feel his health slipping. (He had already lost his sight and couldn't stand sunlight or exposure to the wind, which made him sneeze.) So he resolved to leave the earth's surface for good. . . . He summoned the bull, and with his clammy, feverish hand made a scornful and discouraging gesture, consigning all existence to the depths of nothingness, saying:

"The time has come. I can be happy only underground. My health and joy depend on the slimy underworld. I'm leaving to you, in recognition of your good service, my wife, my belongings, my drums; and I leave you everything unconditionally. You'll be king of Cocozumba when the time comes, or perhaps even earlier if you decide to hurry things up. Live happily on the earth. If at times you feel the need to see your old master out of gratitude, just use your hoof to dig into the earth. Perhaps Earthworm can give you some advice. Or search within yourself to discover what I would do. You can always count on me. Adieu, my son!"

Dingadingá was listening to his words while mending a housecoat but did not raise her eyes from her work nor do anything to dissuade her husband from his plans. Nor did the loyal bull (because of his obedient spirit). And the king and the queen, when they were brought in and consulted, couldn't have been happier about the earthworm's decision, for he was giving them a wonderful successor, an exceptionally gifted bull.

"Indeed," said the queen absentmindedly, "my daughter's husband did win the contest fair and square, but after all, he's only an earthworm. How disgusting!"

As for the king, every time he met the little runt with his hesitant manner, his fearful expression of frightened sadness, his pale and flabby body, always quivering and trembling, he could hardly contain himself. And what really put him over the edge was that syrupy melancholic look that had taken up permanent residence in his eyes. The king could hardly contain the outburst of curses that could give him relief, but only temporarily, from the wrath that the worm's presence, infirmities, and family relationship aroused in him.

Now, here's what happened next. Earthworm disappeared by reducing his volume and taking on the shape that suited him so well, the shape that we all know now and find so disgusting. (You must understand that he was a little white man with fine features; thin, bitter lips; and a narrow moustache. He was bald and barrel-chested, and had short arms and legs, so short that it always seemed like he was sitting down when he was really standing up, thrusting out his corseted torso. Besides, there was always something ailing him.) Anyway, as soon as Earthworm was gone, the first thing the bull did was hang the king from an elm tree and leave him for the moths to eat.

As for the queen, he shut her up in a stinking cell (a dungeon or a latrine, no one knows for sure), where she spent a long time with no food. The poor woman, once she had eaten all the cockroaches covering the walls and the soft floor of her prison (she would suck the cream from their bellies after tearing off and tossing away their legs, wings, and antennas with disgust), she was reduced to eating herself, beginning with her feet, which are so difficult to chew. And that's how she died, poisoned, with utmost indignation. Then the bull donned the crown of parrot feathers, hung the necklaces around his neck, and began to reign at his ease.

Every year, Dingadingá gave him a son, but one woman wasn't enough for him, nor were five, nor even ten. And so he declared that all the women of Cocozumba would now be rightfully his own. There were a few feeble protests here and there. To prevent other protests from developing and spreading a bad example, he gave the order to execute (and named himself executioner) all the men of the kingdom, including his own sons. From then on, whenever one of his many concubines gave birth to a male child, he would scold her, punish her severely, and then slit the baby's throat.

Now the poor women, who had no idea how to avoid sometimes giving birth to boys, went through some tough times. But they eventually got used to it. The bull-king would kill several thousand of his sons every year, and his custom was to climb along with the sun to the top of a hill that stood high above the valleys. There, he would stand proudly at the top, bellowing out his glorious challenge:

"Me, Me, Me, Me, Me
There's not a man in the country but me, me, me!"

The only affirming response came from the kneeling women, his long-suffering herd of women.

Then the bull would come down in triumph and take up his daily routine, absolutely certain that no one would ever challenge him.

Sanune, a stubborn woman the color of roasted almonds, was weaving a basket.

She had had six children. With her very own eyes, burning as they watched, she had seen all six throats slit with a knife, seen them dragged by the foot and thrown into the garbage hole like so many dead cats! Each time, she had dropped the basket she was weaving, in the midst of her pain and anguish, to wash away the blood shed so copiously by her innocent children, the poor cursed fruit of her womb. She was sick and tired of the way things were. So tired that when she realized that she was pregnant for the seventh time (it would be a boy, she was certain), she didn't tell anyone. In Cocozumba there were swarms of spies and tattletales who told the bull about the slightest things his wives did. They were mostly old women who spied diligently on the younger ones, and they seemed to enjoy tormenting them for the slightest reason. No one could be trusted.

It's worth pointing out that Sanune, although she had already had a number of children, was still an adolescent with small firm breasts and a svelte body. Nothing betrayed her, not her easy graceful movements, not even her stomach, for it was remarkably flat given the situation. One day, pretending she had a toothache, she went straight to the bull and asked, with her voice that could a melt a stone, permission to go to the creek. There were lilies there, she said, that could give healing powers to the waters because they had bloomed after the full moon. Scarcely paying attention, the bull answered:

"Very well, go ahead, Sanune. And get better."

It's true that Sanune wasn't really subservient, but she was afraid. She hated the bull and couldn't hide her hate any longer. Given her situation, she absolutely needed to be somewhere she could scream out her hate without anyone's hearing, where she could safely threaten her enemy, and where she could finally feel alone, totally alone and rebellious. However, she didn't go to the creek, but rather to the other side of the river. She crossed the old, abandoned bridge as quickly as in a dream and continued walking on the other side. She came to the edge of the fearsome forest, guided by the spirit of her mother who, while she was alive, was a faithful servant of the saints of iron, her protectors (arrow, bow, nail, chain, and lock), Ogún and Ochosí, Saint Peter and Saint Norbert.[4]

Because Ogún was a man of the forest who lived in solitude. He lived so alone that he actually was the forest. He knew of nothing but animals – his dog's eyes – and plants. Whenever he saw a human being, he would hide. Also, Ogún was a virgin. One day a woman came into the forest, Ochún, la Caridad del Cobre, lady of the rivers, the springs, and the lakes. Did Ochún take a fancy to Ogún? Yes! In fact, she tried to tempt the solitary Ogún and catch him. That was her mission. Ogún ran off without even looking at her, and Ochún chased after him. When she caught up with him where he was hiding in the bush, he turned on her like a wounded wild animal. He roared his threats without deigning to look at her, but that didn't frighten her in the least.

Ochún filled an "*ibá*"[5] with honey while Ogún was hiding in a tree trunk. Then she danced around the tree, and as she danced, she told Ogún:

---

4. In the Lucumí religion, Ogún is a saint (*orisha*) who controls iron and war. He is represented in the Catholic religion as Saint Peter (*San Pedro*) but also as Saint Paul and Saint John the Baptist. Ochosí is an *orisha* who is portrayed as a hunter, a physician, and a seer. He is often represented by an arrow and is a helper to the god Obatalá (the father of *orishas* and creator of humankind). Saint Norbert is the Catholic equivalent.

5. Ibá is her sacred calabash (*jícara*).

"Iyá oñió oñí abbé
Cheketé oñí o abbé."

And that made Ogún want to look at her to see if she was really like he imagined her in her song. He squeezed out of the
trunk, and as soon as he appeared, Ochún rubbed his lips
with honey (oñí). Then Ogún, calmed by the sudden sweetness on his mouth, followed Ochún, who continued singing
and dancing and holding out the honey before him:

"Iyá oñí o oñiadó
Iyá oñí o oñiadó
Iyá loun loro euy loun loro osa oñiaddo."

"Ogún, come out of the forest. With this sweetness that I'm
giving you, with this sweetness that I myself am giving you,
Ogún, come on out of the forest. Because you are the one who
can open and close the heavens, I give you this sweetness so
that you may get inside all saints and all men."

And that's how she led him – attracting him, avoiding him,
charming him – far from the forest. But the forest came along
with him – all the way to Babá's house. Babá kept him prisoner for a while with an iron chain greased with corojo[6] oil
and honey from bees.

Ochosí is the purifier. He is an important saint! Ochosí can
remove bad thoughts and send evil back where it came from.
He can even raise the dead with honey from bees. He's a
miracle worker, Oñí, the lord of the forest and indeed the forest itself. He's the ax, the arrow, and the knife.

Ochosí never knew his mother. He grew up hidden in the

6. The *corojo* is a Cuban tree that produces an oil used in Santeria rituals
(likely *Gastrococos crispa*, although Cabrera lists it in *El Monte* as *Acreemia
crispa*).

forest, and that's where he learned how to use iron. He wore a wildcat's skin and carried a purse full of gold.

He has the personality of a man who is always in love and always loved. Ochosi's laughs are the morning bells. It's true that he never gives any money to his women – except when he's in a really good mood, and you can't count on that – but none of them has ever gone hungry. For them he hunts partridges, guinea fowl, pigeons, doves. They always have plenty of food, because Ochosí is the protector of women; he is their strength, and they all adore him.

But he loves one of them more than the others, and that woman is the mistress of creation and the sea, Yemayá, the Virgin of Regla, the mother of all the saints, who had secretly read the records kept by Orúmbila, the Seer of All.[7] (Orúmbila gave Yemayá to Ochosí because he wanted nothing to do with a woman who knew more than he, and he went back to the sweet golden Ochún.)

Whenever an unhappy woman entreats him, Ochosí always lends an ear and comes to her aid. Attached to one of her ankles, Sanune was wearing a little copper chain that her mother had put there when she was little. Her mother, the daughter of Ogún and the servant of Ochosí, was leading her that day through the forest. Sanune couldn't see her, couldn't feel the pressure of her hand, didn't suspect that she was there. The deceased woman begged for help from Ogún and Ochosí, and the forest opened its arms. . . .

Sanune stopped suddenly, frightened that she had come so far.

7. Yemayá is the goddess of the sea and the moon. She is the archetypical mother, generous and giving. Yemayá is the owner of the collective subconscious and ancient wisdom, since she holds the secrets that are hidden in the sea. She is often invoked in fertility rites and in any ritual concerning women's issues. Orúmbila (Orúnmila, Orula, Ifá) is a divinity in the Yoruba tradition, corresponding to Saint Francis of Assisi in the Catholic tradition.

Two big, proud, handsome black men, black as black deepened by time and as rich as the blue in the sky, appeared before her.[8] One was carrying a gun and was followed by a dog and a stag with a cross on his forehead. The other was armed with a bow and arrow and wore a wildcat skin over one shoulder and an apron called a *wabbi*.

Sanune touched the earth and kissed it on her fingertips. Prostrate at the men's feet, she lost consciousness. When she opened her eyes, she was surrounded by night, in a room thick with the smell of warm foliage and guavas, as if a crowd of blacks had just gathered there a few minutes before. She found herself before an altar made of two wildcat skins and two freshly cut poplar branches propped against the wall. On the ground she could see several soup tureens with their lids on, a horseshoe, two huge pots of rice, some red beans, and popcorn. Beside her, an old woman with her head wrapped in a veil held in her kerchief twenty-one little snails, all beautifully white like unpolished ivory, and she kept counting and re-counting them for fear that one might be lost (specifically the one belonging to Elegguá).[9] When she was convinced that none were missing, she touched Sanune's shoulder and sent her off, giving her a bundle of multicolored clothes.

Some months went by, and Sanune calculated the days that she still had until her baby would be born. On the first day of the last week, she pulled Changó's[10] red cloth out of the bundle, brought it to her lips, inscribed her request on the cloth, and placed it at the foot of a poplar tree.

8. The phrase "black as black deepened by time and as rich as the blue in the sky" appears in the original French version but not in the Spanish.

9. The *orisha* Elegguá, in Yoruba tradition, is a trickster figure, a messenger, and the owner of roads, doors, and opportunities.

10. Changó is the *orisha* of fire and thunder.

Under the musical rustling of the poplar's leaves sits Changó, the world's high priest; without him there is no magic.

On the second day, she went to the seashore and threw in seven copper coins wrapped in Yemayá's blue cloth.

On the third day, she made for the river. Ochún often bathes in the river, and when she leaves the water, all provocative and proud, you need to take her a golden platter with the most exquisite things on it. Those who know how to worship her take fruit down to the river to her. Sometimes Ochún rows her boat in her pumpkin crown. If, out of ignorance or forgetfulness, her follower leaves the offering somewhere else, Ochún flies into a rage and kills him. Sanune gave her tangerines, and then she spread the yellow cloth out on the water and dropped three copper coins, striking terror in a *cayarí*.[11] The sun was precisely in the middle of the sky.

On the fourth day, she roasted some corn. Then, holding three copper coins and Ogún's violet cloth, she threw it on the road using her left hand.

On the fifth day, walking to the left, without anyone seeing her, she tossed Orula's[12] green cloth on the corner of a street that closed off the night.

On the sixth day – taking four steps forward, four steps backward, and always using her left hand – she dropped Odaiburukú's[13] orange cloth in the middle of the crossroads.

And on the seventh day, she called Obatalá[14] and spoke to him through the white cloth, because he can't stand the sun.

11. The *cayarí* is a red shrimp (author's note).

12. Orula (Orúnmila) is an *orisha* known as the adviser to gods and men, often consulted in divination.

13. Odaiburukú may be the same *orisha* as Burukú, the owner of diseases.

14. Obatalá is the father of *orishas*. He represents clarity, justice, and wisdom. Everything that is white on earth belongs to him: snow, sky, bones, and the brain. Sometimes Obatalá is considered an androgynous deity containing both male and female energies.

He works in the shadows. She dipped the cloth in coconut oil and rubbed her stomach with it.

Then she took a bath in an infusion of poplar leaves, artemesia, bay laurel, incense, all of Saint Barbara's herbs, and *siguaraya* boiled in *aguardiente* and bee honey perfumed with tobacco.[15]

At bedtime, she stood over an earthen jar containing a little water and some holy quicksilver and recited the following lines:

"Holy, holy quicksilver, I need you!"

She soon gave birth to a son, and the bull sent her one of his old woman executioners, whose job it was to chop off heads. However, this time, when the old woman plunged her knife into the little calf's neck, Sanune had the strength of mind to conciliate her with a humble smile, offering apologies ("But Mother, whatever am I going to do?") for her thoughtless insistence on disobeying her master's laws.

Scarcely had the horrible woman shuffled off, thinking that her job was finished, than Sanune ran to pull her son's body from the garbage heap and joyously drink some chicken broth.

Then she started weaving her baskets again, smoothly and nimbly, eager to draw attention away from her mistake, and went off into the countryside on the pretext of cutting canes for her weaving. And it was during one of those trips that, hiding it in a basket, she carried her newborn's body into the forest, where Ochosí brought him back to life by rubbing his arms and legs with bee honey. And Ogún said to Sanune:

"Calmly go back to the village. When your son is ten years

15. Santa Barbara is the Catholic saint represented in Santeria rituals as Changó. The *siguaraya* (or *ciguaraya*) is a sacred tree with magical powers (*Trichilia havanensis*). Bathing in an infusion of these herbs guarantees the success of any impossible enterprise (note in the French edition).

old, he'll knock over a palm tree with one thrust of his horns, and when he's twenty, a *ceiba* tree.[16] Then the world will know his voice."

A short time later, she was found dead with a little bell in her hands. Dead, but with a smile on her lips. The more they looked at her, the more difficult it was to believe such a thing possible – how could a corpse be so happy?

Years and years went by.

There were plenty of females born in Cocozumba. According to the bull's wishes, nothing but females. Some grew up and became young women. Others were getting old, and all the old women were dead. Nothing changed in Cocozumba. The only novelty was that after a while, all masculine words not directly related to the bull were eliminated from the language. For example, they would say, "In construction, I use a hammerette" or "I do my cooking on a stovette," and "I cut with my cutlasse." A foot became a "foote," and all masculine words became feminine. No one dared use the masculine word "cielo" for heaven anymore, but rather "ciela."

A surprise hurricane blew through leaving everything topsy-turvy, and people couldn't get its horror out of their minds. They talked for a long time about the "hurricaness" that had reaped so many lives.

The form even of neuter objects became more and more feminized. Never had casseroles been so female or so passive; never had water jugs ever been so sexual with their hips and their hands resting on their hips; nor had earthenware ever been so placid or had such a paunch. Even knives, after days of being called knivettes, had taken on a totally different way of looking. In short, if sometimes the women couldn't avoid sighing "oh my God, my God," on occasion without punishment, it was because the bull believed, and with good reason,

16. The *ceiba* tree (the silk-cotton tree) is considered sacred in Cuba.

that they must be speaking of him. So, in Cocozumba, the only man anyone could speak about was God, given that God and the bull were one and the same. And so he could continue climbing to the top of the hill as morning broke to bellow out his sovereign vanity:

"Me, me, me, me! . . . Me, me, me, me!
There's not another man in the world but me, me, me, me!"

But one morning, after the One and Only, the Peerless One with the final word, the Unique and the Absolute, had proclaimed from the heights his glorious notoriety, there answered a voice from a point on the horizon, on the path of the night! A voice vibrant with strength and with youth, a triumphant male voice, which broke a half-century of adoring silence:

"Me, me, me, me! . . . Me, me, me, me!
I'm Bregantino Bregantín!"

The bull-king was horrified and couldn't stand to suffer the shame of believing his own ears (though he heard perfectly well, and the skin on his back quivered with the chill of that cry as it vibrated like living gold). So while a luminous stupor spread over the four cardinal points of his domain, he stood up tall like a giant, proudly repeating his credo:

"Me, me, me, me! . . . Me, me, me, me!
I recognize no other man in the world but me, me, me, me!"

Meanwhile, the other bull, an imposing fellow, was leaping across valleys, charging recklessly across the countryside, knocking down everything he found in his path. He was especially angry with the palm groves. With his horns, he uprooted royal palms and *ceiba* trees weighted down by the centuries, tossing them over his head. The women squealed, and

17

their unpleasant cackling annoyed the king. Running away from a young bull is the rule, really the rule. Something that's logical and obvious to the most simpleminded. Totally understandable. Common sense dictates running away, especially when the bull looks to you like a walking mountain. Legs normally lend themselves immediately to that kind of reaction. But the people of Cocozumba, still spread out as they were beginning their day's activity, neither individually nor in groups did they put on the show of pell-mell, grotesque flight that normally happens when people try to flee at breakneck speed for their very lives. Indeed, on the contrary, because the population was female to the core and used to suffering – what's one blow more or less? – they went crazy with admiration, and coquettishly cheered the power and the acrobatics of the surprising bull.

> "Me, me, me, me! . . . Me, me, me, me!
> Now I'm the Thick Forest, Thick Forest!"

With a furious, menacing look, the bull-king, filled with hate and vengeance more toward his women than toward the insolent newcomer, measured the distance separating him from his rival. The other was about the same size, had the same regal bearing, and in addition . . . he was young!

Time hung suspended for one horribly beautiful moment!

They rushed at each other, and there in the middle of the plain they raised such a cloud of dust and fire that they were hidden from the women who were eager to watch such a fearsome battle. After all – for that's how the tender hearts of mothers and wives saw things – the battle was being fought in homage to them by these furious, bigger-than-life gentlemen. They heard the terrible attack, the shock of the horns. Their eyes, their hearts were caught up in this whirlwind of bravado. When the explosion quieted, there was the old bull, lying on the ground with fountains of blood gushing from his body. And the young bull was still attacking, exasperated that he couldn't kill him more than once.

Then the women knelt down before the winner and exclaimed:

"You are our master. The Unique. Bregantino Bregantín. There is no man on earth but you, Thick Forest, Thick Forest! Without a master, we could never live!"

But Bregantino had nothing in mind but to put an end to the tyranny that his father had carried out for so long. He thanked them all graciously and allowed them to rub his back without his appearing too proud. And he also went looking for men. One for each woman.

And that's how nature reclaimed its rights and men were again born in Cocozumba.

Chéggue

Chéggue is in the forest with his father, learning how to hunt. Since the New Year is approaching, his father says:

"Hold your arrow! This is a time when we are not allowed to hunt. For just as we celebrate the holidays by having fun in the village, the animals have the right to celebrate in the forest."

They went back down to the village. No one was hunting or spilling the blood of any animal. All the men were staying home quietly.

On New Year's morning, Chéggue woke up in tears.

His mother looked at him and asked:

"Why, Chéggue, why *sukú-sukú?* Why are you crying?

"Because I left my arrow in the forest. I'm crying for my lost arrow."

Iyaré (the mother) went to tell her husband that Chéggue was crying because his arrow was still in the forest.

The father answered:

"Now is not the time to go back there, nor the time to handle an arrow."

But Chéggue kept weeping and saying that he wouldn't eat anything until he got his arrow back.

"Let him go get his arrow," begged Iyaré.

"All right, he can go," agreed the father. "If something bad happens to us, it'll be your fault, Iyaré."[1]

So Chéggue goes off into the forest. He picks up his arrow.

He sees a large group of animals busy eating and drinking hot *dengue*.[2]

---

1. This sentence is in the French edition but not in the Spanish edition.
2. *Dengue* is a hot drink made from corn (author's note).

He throws his arrow, and it buries itself in the heart of the oldest animal of all.

❧

Chéggue doesn't come back from the forest.

Iyaré, with a group of women, goes looking for him. Under the trees, the women begin calling:

> "Chéggue, oh, Chéggue!
> Chéggue, oh, Chéggue!"

Chéggue does not answer. But the animals do, and they answer in chorus.

The women cannot understand what they are saying. They go to get the men. The men understand.

Chéggue's father steps forward, alone.

> "Chéggue, oh, Chéggue!
> Chéggue, oh, Chéggue!"

And then all the animals appear, dancing and singing:

> "Chéggue, oh, Chéggue!
> Tanike Chéggue nibe ún
> Chéggue ono chono ire ló
> Chéggue up the creek!"

"Chéggue saw us joyously celebrating the New Year. With an arrow he killed our chief. With an arrow to the heart. Chéggue is dead. His body is over there, in the creek."

"Come," said the hunter to Iyaré. "Chéggue lies dead in the creek."

And he picked him up and carried him away on his shoulders.

Eyá

Once there was a fisherman.

It had been a long time since any fish had wanted to bite on his hook. They would just steal his bait and make fun of him.

Whenever he pulled his nets in, nothing! Just trash. So he put aside his gear and stopped fishing.

One morning, his wife said to him:

"Today you have to bring me a nice fat red snapper or a plump prawn."

"That's impossible," he replied. "The tide is out."

"You're just a good-for-nothing!" she answered. "The whole neighborhood is waiting to buy fish from you, and you won't even go down to the seashore."

"That's because the fish aren't biting," the fisherman protested. "Someone has cast a spell on me."

"Bring me back something – even just a measly sardine – if you don't want me to die!" she shouted.

The man went down to the sea and pushed off from the shore. He pulled his line back in with a lovely, big fish, who said:

"Don't kill me!"

"I don't really want to kill you," answered the fisherman, "but my wife said that she has to eat some fish or she'll die."

"Throw me back into the water, and I'll fill up three boatloads of fish for you."

He threw it back, and the fish fulfilled its promise. And the fisherman walked through the village, calling out:

"Eyá é! Eyá é!"

Eyá means fish (author's note).

He sold everything. He kept the biggest fish for his own household. When the fish was cooked and served on a platter, the fisherman said to his wife:

"Do you see how fat and lovely this fish is? Well, it's the only one left of the three boatloads that the first fish I caught brought me."

Then the woman slammed it down, shouting:

"This isn't the fish I want. I want the one you caught first."

"That wouldn't be right," said the man. "That fish helped me make so much money!"

"I don't care," replied the woman. "If you don't want me to die, you must bring it back to me tomorrow."

The next day, he went back out to sea. The water was so clear that you could see all the way to the bottom, just like looking through a windowpane. You could even see heaven's roots. The same fish came back, took the hook, and there it was at the end of the line, brilliant as a jewel.

"Alas!" said the fisherman. "Today, I have to take you home. You're the fish my wife wants to eat. If she doesn't eat you, she will die. She has never told a lie."

"Leave me here in the sea! If you do, I'll fill up your boat for you six times over with fish."

The man accepted, then returned home calling:

"Eyá, Eyá eé eyá dé!"

Back at his own home, he had with him a huge fish, twice as large as the first one.

"There," he said, once they were sitting around the table. "That's the fish that I have left from the six boatloads that the first fish I caught brought me."

"Well, I don't want that fish either!" shouted the woman, throwing the fish down. "Tomorrow if you don't bring me back the first one you caught, tomorrow, you understand, I'll surely die."

How sad the fisherman was as he rowed his boat. The same fish came back, stuck its golden head out of the water, and said to him:

"I know that I must die today. Take me. But when you are back home, plant my gills at the foot of the *obbí*, the coconut tree. Give my entrails to your dog, Ayabé Kúmbele, and have the mare eat my tail."

"I will," said the fisherman.

Three days later, the woman, who had eaten Eyá, gave birth to three sons. The dog had three puppies, and the mare had three colts. The three boys stood up and said to their mother:

"*Iyá mí!*"[1]

Then they ran out and went straight to the coconut tree. There they dug up three lances. They went to the dog and took her three puppies; to the mare, and took her three colts. Then they went back to their mother and began to dance around her, waving their lances and chanting:

"Ayambe kúmbele koima!
Abe kún kua neye. Eh! allambé kúmbele koima!
Abe kún Kuaniyé!"

And off they ran, into the forest.

In Africa, so say the old men, the names of those three are:

Taeguo, Kaínde, and Oddúo.

1. *Iyá mí* means "my mother" (author's note).

Walo-Wila

There were two sisters: Walo-Wila and Ayere Kénde (sometimes called Kénde Ayere). Walo-Wila never went out in public. No one had ever seen her.

Ayere Kénde would sit on the balcony. Leaning on the railing, Ayere Kénde would enjoy the cool of the evening sea breeze.

Then a wooden horse, a musical horse, came by. He said:
"Please, a drink of water."

Ayere Kénde had a golden goblet. She filled it with water and gave it to the horse.

"Oh, what a lovely goblet, Ayere Kénde," he said. "I've never seen a prettier one in all my life."

"Yes, but my sister is more beautiful, much more beautiful!"

"Well then, I want to see her, Ayere Kénde. Let me come in."

"If you marry her, you will see her then, my brother," said Ayere Kénde.

Walo-Wila was living and dying behind the drawn blinds, living and dying. . . .

Kénde Ayere sang out:

> "Walo-Wila, Walo Kénde,
> Ayere Kénde,
> You've got a visitor, Kénde Ayere!"

> Walo-Wila asked:
> "Walo-Wila, Walo Kénde,
> Ayere Kénde,
> Who's the visitor, Kénde Ayere?"

"Walo-Wila, Walo Kénde,
Ayere Kénde,
It's Br'er Horse, Kénde Ayere."

"Walo-Wila, Walo Kénde,
Ayere Kénde,
What does Br'er Horse want, Kénde Ayere?"

"Walo-Wila, Walo Kénde,
Ayere Kénde,
He wants a wedding, Kénde Ayere."

"Walo-Wila, Walo Kénde,
Ayere Kénde,
Tell Br'er Horse that I'm ugly, Kénde Ayere."

"Walo-Wila, Walo Kénde,
Ayere Kénde,
Tell him that I've only one eye, Kénde Ayere."

"Walo-Wila, Walo Kénde,
Ayere Kénde,
That I'm swollen up, Kénde Ayere."

"Walo-Wila, Walo Kénde,
Ayere Kénde,
That I'm rotten through and through. Kénde Ayere!"

"So long. Good-bye," said the horse.

Ayere Kénde stayed on her balcony. Goat-Man, Bull-Man, and Turtle-Man came by. Then Tiger-Man, Elephant-Man, and Lion-Man. They were thirsty. They all asked for a drink. When Ayere Kénde filled up the fine gold goblet for them, they all admired it, and she always said:

"My sister hiding behind the blinds is more beautiful."

And they all wanted to see her, but Walo-Wila would sing from behind the blinds:

> "Alas! How ugly I am!
> I've only one eye!
> How twisted my legs are!
> And how mangy I am!"

And off they would go in disgust.

Stag, the son of Honeysuckle, hadn't drunk from the golden goblet.

Ayere Kénde was on her balcony enjoying the cool of the evening, rocking in her rocking chair. . . . And off in the distance, her eyes were dreaming. . . .

Stag came up and said:

"Ayere Kénde, give me some water in your golden goblet."

She filled the cup and gave it to him.

"I've never seen anything so beautiful," exclaimed Stag.

"Oh, more beautiful yet, much more beautiful yet, is my sister whom no one has ever seen."

"Show me, Ayere Kénde. I'll be able to see her."

"You do have sweet eyes. If you marry her, you'll be able to see her, my brother. Wait. Just wait."

> "Walo-Wila, Walo Kénde,
> Ayere Kénde,
> You've got a visitor, Kénde Ayere."

And Walo-Wila answered, sad as the dusk at her window:

> "Tell him that I'm ugly,
> That I'm a cripple,
> That I've got only one eye,
> That I'm all swollen up. . . .

"I'll marry her!" repeated the stag.

Then Walo-Wila declared:

"The mother of my sister lives at the bottom of the sea. The mother of my sister is Kariempémbe."

At midnight, Walo-Wila gave Ayere Kénde a gourd filled with pearls.

Ayere Kénde tossed out the pearls. Then she called Stag over and gave him the gourd, saying:

"Go down to the bottom of the sea."

Stag ran to the shore, and the whole seashore was in song:

"Walo-Wila, Walo-Wila, Walo-Wila, Walo-Wila!"

Then he entered the water through the slit made by the knife of the moon.

Ayere Kénde waited all night on her balcony. At dawn, Stag returned. His gourd was filled to the brim with blue water, filled with the sapphires of Olokun.[1]

And Ayere Kénde said to him:

"Go into my sister's bedroom."

Walo-Wila was more beautiful, far more beautiful than Ayere Kénde's goblet.

When the moon and the sea kiss . . .

---

1. The *orisha* Olokun corresponds to Our Lady of Regla.

Two Queens

Once there were two queens. Two Lucumí queens.[1] They lived across from each other. One's name was Eléren Güedde, and the other Oloya Gúanna.

Eléren Güedde was an excellent cook. Both were quite rich, but Oloya Gúanna didn't like to spend her money. She would go to her friends' houses to eat. She often ate with Eléren Güedde. But finally one day Eléren Güedde got tired of being taken advantage of.

"Listen to what I have to say," said Eléren Güedde, "listen, Oloya Gúanna: The person who shares always thinks it is a lot, even if it is not much at all. But the person who is on the receiving end always thinks it is not very much, even when it is a lot. That I know for a fact."

So, one day, the queen Eléren Güedde stood at her door, and when the queen Oloya Gúanna showed up singing

> Eléren Güedde guola tóa,
> Eléren Güedde guola tóa!

she said:

"Uguaka Maka! Just wait till I smash your face in!"

And she beat her silly.

The result? A real war. But Queen Oloya Gúanna no longer comes to have dinner with Queen Eléren Güedde, and every day they face off and scratch each other's eyes out.

That's the story of Queen Eléren Güedde and Queen Oloya Gúanna.

1. In Cuba the word Lucumí refers to the Yoruba people and their culture and religion. See Jorge Castellanos and Isabel Castellanos, *Cultura Afrocubana* (Miami: Ediciones Universal, 1988), vol. 4, 28–29.

Papa Turtle and Papa Tiger

Back in the days when the world was young, the frog had hair and put it up in curlers. In the beginning, everything was green. Not only the leaves and the grass and everything else that's still green today, like the lime and the grasshopper, but also all the rocks, the animals, and man, whom Oba-Ogó[1] created by blowing on his doodoo.

But everything then was still a little chaotic. The fish drank from flowers and the birds built their nests on the crests of the waves. Oceans poured out of seashells, and rivers from the corners of the eyes of the first sad crocodile.

Mosquito dug his stinger into the rump of the mountain, and the whole mountain range began to quiver. And that's the day the elephant married the ant. A man climbed up to heaven on a ray of light. The sun was watching, and said:

"Don't get too close or I'll scorch you."

But the man didn't listen. He got too close, was roasted, and turned black from his head to his toes. That was the first black man, the father of all black people. (Blacks are joyous by nature.)

Hicotea (Jicotea) is the Cuban word for turtle. Lydia Cabrera, in her book *El Monte* (102), says about the turtle: "Al principio, la Jicotea, . . . era un hombre, exactamente igual que todos les hombres" (in the beginning, the Turtle was a man exactly like all other men).

1. Oba-Ogó. The god Obatalá is a Yoruba god of creation. Cabrera's words are instructive here: "Olofi, Oloru, Obbá-Oloru . . . Sambi: concepto de un dios supremo 'en el que ya nadie piensa,' un ser misterioso, vago, inconcebible . . . Y ajeno enteramente a cuanto sucede en la tierra" [Olofi, Oloru, Obbá-Oloru . . . Sambi: the concept of a supreme god, about whom nobody thinks, mysterious, vague, inconceivable . . . and totally oblivious to everything that happens on earth]. (*Páginas sueltas*, 303)

Another man went to the moon on a horse-bird-cayman-cloudlet. The moon has a single round eye, in a circle painted with charcoal. And in its eye there's a hare turning in circles.

Now that eye is a cold-water cistern, full of the sky's primordial water. And the hare is an ice fish. Rain dwells in the moon's eye.

The moon was stillborn. Neither man nor woman. Chaste. When its mother realized that she had given birth to nothing more than a flat tin-plate face, to a corpse's head, she had a nervous breakdown. To calm her, the father massaged her with elderberry flowers and called her Moon, saying:

"Moon, be born, die, and come back to life."

The moon rolled down the mountain. It went deep into the forest, where the hare was trying to strike fire with a smooth pebble.

The moon said to the hare:

"Run, tell men for me that just as I am born, die, and come back to life, they too must be born, die, and come back to life."

The hare took off to look for men and the moon stayed behind on a tuft of reeds to wait.

Along the way, the hare met his cousin the agouti drinking beer. He had swiped a keg, and he was drunk, dead drunk.

"Let me taste some," said the hare.

He wasn't used to drinking. The beer went straight to his head and scrambled the message the moon had entrusted to him.

When he came back on wobbly legs, the moon asked:

"What did you tell the men?"

"Ha, ha, ha!" I said, "Just as I am born, die, and, uh, don't come back to life, you too must be born, die, and not come back to life." And so they began digging their graves. . . .

The moon grabbed the hare by the ears and whacked him across the mouth with a bamboo stick.

"As your punishment," she said, "I'm going to keep you prisoner forever." And she locked him in her only eye with a good silver padlock. Since then, much as he might run in circles trying to find a way out, he can't escape.

The moon is cold. Cold is white. The man who went to the moon turned white. And that was the first white man, the father of all white people. They are sad. . . . There's a reason for everything.

"Let's be brothers," Turtle said back then to the stag, called "Legs of Wind."

"Fine," answered the stag.

"Let's always stay together," added Turtle.

"Fine," answered the stag.

So they followed the same road together. They came to a lake. There they fished out the evening star with a net and went to look for the king's daughter, Anikosia, and gave it to her, still dripping wet. With delight, the king's daughter hung it from her ear. She was cross-eyed and her belly hung down to her knees. She had only one breast, which was long, really long, and thin. She would throw it over her shoulder for convenience, and it still dragged on the ground. Though she was still a virgin, her inexhaustible supply of milk fed all of her father Masawe's subjects.

She gave Turtle and the stag some ivory and gold, but she didn't like the star, her new glowing earring. What she really wanted was Turtle's blood, because it could cure asthma. However, Anikosia's eye said:

"I'll make a lasso."

And Turtle's eye heard her and replied:

"I'll make a knife."

And the two eyes laughingly challenged each other like teeth.

Then the king's daughter said:

"Let's run away. I can't go home to my father because I stole his gold and his ivory."

"Fine," said Legs-of-Wind.

"Let's not waste any time. It won't be long before the rooster, who guards the king's treasury, tells on me."

They left without anyone seeing them, crossing the square where the blind were sunning themselves, killing each others' fleas and munching on them with delight.

Anikosia led the way, and when she thought they were far enough away from her father's lands, out of range of her father's initial burst of anger (often his anger made for some very nice cataclysms that could change the face of the earth), they stopped to rest under a leafy *jagüey*.[2]

Anikosia lay down and pretended to fall immediately into the deep sleep of the weary. Stag stretched out next to her; however, Anikosia fell asleep right away. Turtle grabbed the woman's breast, which was crawling along the ground like a snake – osí, osé, osé – and tied it tightly to the trunk of the *jagüey* tree. Then he pulled out his machete, which rang out like a silver bell filled with the light of dawn, and he woke up Stag, yelling:

"This woman's face is too ugly. We have to cut off her head!"

And with one fell swoop, he severed the head from the body.

Anikosia felt herself being torn apart and tossed into the air like a grapefruit, so violently and with so little warning that it took her a couple seconds to realize how serious her situation

2. A *jagüey* is a Cuban tree (*Ficus membranacea*).

was. She was stunned and dazed by the sudden explosion of lights, by the deafening outburst like bells in her head, by the whistles and buzzing that were set off inside her when she crashed against a stone. But then, once she had recovered from that first horrible, unexpected shock, she pulled herself together with an indescribable rush, outraged to the core of her gray matter. Then, she fell on Turtle, ferociously biting the protrusions of his shell. She broke all four rows of her sharp, pointy teeth and wrecked her jaw. She was so frustrated by this new obstacle that she couldn't stop to think calmly, so she pounded Turtle's hard, invincible armor, using her forehead, her temples, and her skull until she did herself in and fell like a rotten fruit, defeated by her own rage, at the feet of her impassible executioner.

Meanwhile, a new head, with an even more repulsive face and awful grimace, was growing on Anikosia's shoulders, just behind where her old head had been. (And throughout the fight, her two arms had not stopped desperately trying to pull the captive breast loose. But pulling only tightened the knot that held it.) Once again, Turtle sliced off her head cleanly, striking right at her Adam's apple. This head didn't have enough strength to bite or attack. Instead, it was content to show its hatred with some very expressive evil looks and a few nasty words. Then, a swarm of black moths flew out of her mouth. They were horned *tataguas*,[3] and they had Anikosia's flashing eyes and face stamped on the funeral-black velvet of their wings.

A third head grew, but it barely had time to show its nose and old, wrinkly forehead before Anikosia's body, still convulsing discreetly, lay down and finally died once and for all.

Turtle and Legs-of-Wind watched as the golden leaf of an unknown plant grew up through the corpse's navel. Driven by

3. The *tatagua* is a large nocturnal moth (*Erebus odorata*).

their curiosity, they opened her belly and discovered the seeds and roots of plants that had never yet been planted, including the first kernel of corn, like a kernel of sunshine.

They headed off in the direction marked by the grasses bending in the wind. Legs-of-Wind carried the body until they could find a suitable burial place. As they left the green land, the earth began to crack with drought and rear up. When they came to the edge of the precipice, they threw the corpse over the edge. But the *tataguas* that had sprung from the lips and breath of Anikosia's second head flew off to tell the king what had happened, and now they were coming back by the millions, blocking out the light of day. The walls of the horizon they had left behind them began to tremble and crumbled down in a silent crash.

Stag thought he saw the shadow of an enormous hunter, and in his heart, fear made him sense the growing impatience of the pack of dogs ready to leap on him from the leaden clouds. The dogs had his scent in their nostrils! Turtle, however, realized that the volcanoes would wake up soon.

The heavy, gloomy flight of the *tataguas*, continually dying and being born all over again were drawing the usual signs of malediction in the sky over Turtle's and Stag's heads.

"Legs-of-Wind, my brother," said Turtle as he jumped on his antlers and hung on for dear life, "don't leave me. You're my legs just as I'm your brain! You wouldn't abandon me just when Masawe is planning his vengeance? That devilish old man put smoldering tinder in his volcanoes so that they would vomit their fire out on us!"

Stag fled the loosed dogs, the hunter, and even more than the hunter, the memory of his action, his looming shadow, just as all of Stag's ancestors had fled before it. His ancestors were with him now, inside him, and they all fled together at a speed that only Hurricane can sometimes unleash during his furious campaigns, a speed never equaled by the tidal waves of lava, like the ones spewing out at them now.

And they came to the end of the earth and the beginning of the shining sapphire sea. Kalunga![4]

"Oh, great Mother of my race," begged Turtle, "save the smallest of your children."

And a great mass emerged from the water before them, the giant Morrocoy,[5] diving through the water with grace and majesty. As priest of the ocean, he had rocked it in his arms. With his distinctive character and dressed in rock and algae, he had been a priest since the beginning of time in this deserted coast's sanctuary. But, as he had grown older, he had forgotten the liturgical gestures and now could remember only one of them – the blessing of the water – and he touchingly repeated it over and over again with fervent obstinacy.

Moyumba[6] cannot cross over these endless waters stretching to the sky. . . . Morrocoy's venerable body swam across the seven oceans of seven colors and across a stretch of time, carrying Stag and Turtle. And, in a key moment in the history of the world, he dropped them off one evening on the shore of a blessed island,[7] right around the year 1845. . . .

They were certain that no misfortune could now befall them in this new country that resembled a gentle caress, and they set out into the perfumed forest. They walked and walked and finally came to a big city surrounded by the sea.

The women there were like flowers, and many of the men

4. Kalunga means "Mother Water" and probably refers to the Atlantic Ocean.

5. Morrocoy is a large turtle native to Cuban waters.

6. In the French translation Cabrera authorized the word "Mañunga" and gave the meaning as "*maléfice personnifié*" (malice personified).

7. The "blessed island" is, of course, Cuba.

looked like women with their graceful hips and tiny feet. They were dressed in white and their voices were like honey. Turtle and Legs-of-Wind had gold, ivory, and the seeds from Anikosia's belly, and when they learned that in this new country land wasn't available to whoever claimed it but rather needed to be bought, with gold as the currency, they exchanged their gold for a beautiful property that would later be called Ochú-Kuá-Oru-Okuku.

"Here, we're going to become big landowners," Turtle said to Stag.

"Fine," replied Stag.

In addition to two hats made from palm straw, they got hold of a plow and two new machetes. They prepared a good part of the land and planted the seeds. They worked on with no consideration for Sundays and mandatory holidays, working as hard as they could, planting all sorts of things. And everything came up like magic. It was wonderful. They got rich in no time.

Years and years went by. All that time, living under the good Lord's peace, Turtle and Stag kept themselves busy and enjoyed the fruits of their land. Stag lived in the northernmost part of the property in a little stone house with a tile roof. Turtle lived in the southernmost part. His house always smelled of *piscuales*[8] and jasmine and looked out over the road, where creaky carts and peasants with their animals would pass by. Turtle and Stag were as tight as two peas in a pod, and they couldn't do without one another.

When he came across the sea, Turtle had brought sorcery with him, hidden in his pupil, along with the art of healing with herbs, sticks, and songs.

8. *Piscuales* are climbing plants with very sweet-smelling flowers (*Quiscualis indica*).

One day, the stag fell ill.

For a long time, Turtle had been so busy planting and harvesting the fields that he no longer took the time to reflect on worldly matters. It just so happened, on this occasion, that when he climbed to the top of a hill to look for certain herbs he needed to make a potion for his friend, he stopped – possibly longer than was good for Stag's future – to contemplate the incredible fertile expanse of Ochú-Kuá-Oru-Okuku that stretched out before him. For the first time, he felt a very strong new emotion.

"Owning the whole is not the same as owning half," was the thought that ran through that landowner's mind up there on the hill. At his feet flourished acres of palm groves, virgin forests of cedars and mahogany trees, fields of golden corn, manioc, and, off in the distance, ripening rice in the glistening lagoons. For the first time, his heart filled with greed for the land, and his greed was as big as the day. He thought painfully and greedily about the thousands upon thousands of pieces of fruit ripening at that very moment on every tree in the orchard. He wanted to have them all for himself, the avocados, guavas, and plums his brother had planted. The honey-sweet oranges, famous throughout the land; the mangoes from which you could drink warm melted sunshine; the star apples, whose luscious deep purple color made you think of a black woman's lips; the sapodillas, whose rough skin protected a heart so sweet that memories of their succulence brought water to his mouth; the *sapotes* and the sweet soursops, which already weighed down the branches with their ripeness, hanging juicy and swollen like the breasts of a pregnant woman.[9] As it was, the whole of Ochú-Kuá-Oru-Okuku

9. In the French text, the word used for star apples is the Spanish *caïmitos*; in the Spanish text, the word *caminitos* is surely a misprint. The scientific name is *Chrysolphyllum cainito*. In Spanish, sapodillas are *nísperos*; the scien-

was only half his. As Turtle relaxed in the breeze on the hilltop, happily breathing in the lemon-soaked air, and identifying the scent of each breath of air from his fields, he got carried away by his thoughts and lost track of his conscience's clear, deep voice.

He resolved to give up his hunt for the herbs he was seeking to ward off the evil fever demons – including even Burukú[10] himself – by blocking access to the blood. You need real skill and perseverance to find them because they can change their shape and position at the slightest sound. One glance at them without Ifá[11] is all they need to escape by blending in with the bushes, hiding in a crack in the rocks, or flying off higher and farther than a vulture. In inexperienced hands, uninitiated by a true sorcerer of the night or by the sons and grandsons of Babalá's own grandsons, the herbs could turn into thin air. Instead, Turtle turned to the heavens and fervently called down a curse.

The refreshing thought that his faithful friend might soon croak brought pure joy to his heart. So, as soon as the pink of the evening fell upon the palm groves, rather than sending him the herbs that bring life from life, Turtle sent Stag – who lay shivering from fever in his hammock, anxiously awaiting his friend's return – three Chicherekús. The Chicherekús were wooden dolls or ancient stillborn babies with worn, smooth faces and no eyes or nose, only a hungry mouth with

tific name is *Manilkara zapota*. In Spanish, *sapotes* are *mameyes*; the scientific name is *Pouteria sapota*. In Spanish, soursops are *guanábanas*; the scientific name is *Annona muricata*.

10. Burukú is a demon who causes convulsions and kills through smallpox (author's note). The Yoruba word "burùkù" means "bad."

11. Ifá is the Yoruba god of wisdom and divination, and also refers to a system of divination. At the same time, it is the sum of all knowledge and wisdom in Santeria or La Regla Lucumí.

pearly white teeth. They waved knives or *guayacan*[12] sticks, flit-
ted about springing from the shadows, and endlessly mocked
and harassed him, showing off their teeth:

"Daddy! Mommy! Look at my teeth!"

They tormented him all night with their hellish, piercing
shrieks. Again and again, they brought him to the brink, far
beyond nightmares, until the sun (they were children of
darkness) forced them to retreat in fear back into the lair they
came from, to die once more in Cunanfinda,[13] back to the
breast of Agayú their creator or back to the Woman Owner of
Evil Things.

The stag spent more than a week like this, his tongue like a
slug dragging itself through the dust or like a dirt path that
he was forever swallowing. With every movement, his bones
ached from all the blows from the Chicherekús.[14] When he lay
still and felt his soul leaving him, he could hear in the pit of
his stomach thick, warm water lapping, water full of rotten
sunshine and so heavy that he couldn't have held himself up.[15]

Turtle never did come back with his potion. If Stag hadn't
finally puked up that water, where fever lay like a lily root or a
black cat, or if he hadn't been holding the charm[16] his mother
had given him, and if Eleddá, a guardian angel, hadn't been at

12. A *guayacan* is a small flowering tropical tree (scientific name *Guiacum
coulteri*).

13. A Cabrera note identifies *Cunanfinda* as a cemetery. Agayí is the father
of Changó, according to Cabrera (*Páginas sueltas*, 300).

14. In the Spanish text, the verb is "*moría*" instead of "*movía*." Although it
seems that the verb "to move" is more logical in this context, the idea
of death does appear in the following sentence. Therefore another reading
might be "whenever he died."

15. In the French version, the idea is a bit different. There, "his other
body, the body that doesn't die, was leaving him" ("son autre corps, – celui
qui ne passe pas, – l'abandonnait").

16. The word used for charm is the Cuban vernacular *resguardo*.

his side – he would surely have died right then and there, and not later, when it was his time.

He made a quick recovery by eating eggs and drinking chicken broth. He was sure that Turtle must also be sick – and that's why he hadn't come. So as soon as Stag was back on his feet, he climbed on his horse and galloped across the property, anxious to see how his friend was doing. There he found Turtle, bursting with health, smoking a cigar under his porch roof.

The stag's hurt pierced him through and through, and he cried:

"Hello, brother! I just about died from a nasty fever."

Turtle acted like he wasn't even there. Not only did he ignore his greeting, but he went so far as to turn scornfully the other way and spit – the way you spit when you do it on purpose, to proclaim an insult rather than simply suggest one.

Legs-of-Wind was baffled by Turtle's worrisome behavior, by that unfair and hurtful gesture of spitting intentionally. Turtle's actions cut him to the quick.

"I wonder what I've done to hurt my brother?" the stag thought. Since he wasn't one of those people who are always so sure of themselves, he naturally blamed himself for mistakes he couldn't even remember making. Dismayed, he said:

"Hello, brother, hello. Good day to you. What have I done to deserve such a welcome?"

Turtle stretched out as best he could his yellow and black striped neck, and deigned to respond in a scornful tone that matched his earlier silence.

"Shouldn't you perhaps be the one who greets me first and pays your respects to me?"

"And . . . on what grounds, brother? I . . . You . . ."

"On the grounds that, up until now, things have not been as they should be. I just had never realized it! My reasons are not open to discussion. And the first reason is that I, Master Turtle-Turtle, am superior to you."

Drawing upon what little was left of his self-esteem, Legs-of-Wind feebly replied:

"No, I don't think so! I disagree."

"You must greet me first."

Hardly knowing what to say, Stag stammered:

"But . . . no!"

"And from now on, you'll show me the proper respect."

"No! . . . No way!"

"Fine," said Turtle, his mind made up. He stood up, adjusted his pants, which were always too baggy, and continued:

"Let's see who is more of a man and who's the boss."

But it didn't come down to a fight, as the mockingbird, who had stopped warbling from the top of the sugar apple tree[17] so he could watch what was happening down below, originally thought it would.

"We'll each cut down a section of the forest. Whoever finishes first will be master over the whole domain, and there will be no disputing the outcome. That means whoever wins will be the one and only master."

"Fine," Legs-of-Wind sadly agreed.

It was Sunday, a day when our friends Turtle and Legs-of-Wind usually pulled on their striped linen pants and donned their fine embroidered shirts and silk scarves to be admired by all in the village. But today, instead of flirting with the young women or playing cards or watching their cocks fight in the pit, they sharpened their machetes and went off to clear their respective lands. Br'er Stag chopped and chopped! And Br'er

17. In Spanish, the sugar apple tree is called *anón*. The scientific name is *Annona squamosa*.

Turtle chopped and chopped! Finally, on the fifteenth day, both of them felled the last tree at the very same time.

"Neither you nor I, Br'er Turtle."

"Neither you nor I, Br'er Stag."

That being the case, Turtle decided:

"Let's set fire to our fields. When mine is burning, I'll walk into the flames and will stay there until everything is burned. If I burn up like a small branch, then you'll be the rightful ruler of everything. If – heaven forbid! – you're the one who burns up, then everything that's yours will be mine since you'll be dead. I don't see any other way to settle such a ticklish situation."

"But who's going to risk his life first?" asked Legs-of-Wind, who personally would have preferred settling such a delicate issue by fleeing rather than by roasting.

"Me, naturally," said Turtle haughtily. "I'll sing to you from the middle of the glowing red embers as long as the fire burns, and you can answer me from your cool safe place."

Stag thought it seemed like a fair and reasonable solution. He struck a match to Turtle's felled trees and watched his friend disappear calmly into the burning brush. Now Turtle knew the area, and he went to hide in a cave, carefully blocking its entrance with a rock. The fire came and went, crackling up above. From the safety of his hiding place, he sang:

> "Biribiriquiá, bericó
> Biribiriquiá, bericó.
> Biribiriquiá, bericó!"

The fire burned out and Turtle left the cave. He dragged the rock he had used to block the entrance all the way to the middle of the forest and lay down on it, his belly in the air. That's how Stag found him – smiling, arms crossed behind his head, totally unscathed – as if he had just awoken from a peaceful nap under the mere blaze of a flame-tree's flowers.

"Here's where I faced the challenge, as you can see. A river of fire flowed over me. And my saliva tasted like glowing embers. And I myself probably tasted like fire. I saw red everywhere, but I didn't fry. Be strong, my brother! Now it's your turn to burn a little."

Legs-of-Wind confidently threw himself into the fire. Immediately the flames seized him and swallowed him up until he was nothing but a flame among flames. Ironically, when Turtle sang

> "Biribiriquiá, bericó
> Biribiriquiá, bericó.
> Biribiriquiá, bericó!"

the only response was the crackling of the forest.

Then Turtle went looking for the carbonized remains of his friend in the debris.

"Alas! Legs-of-Wind!" he wept. "My good buddy, my brother! Empty you came into this world . . . !"

He recited an "Our Father" over his body and cut off his antlers, which the fire had licked without destroying.

Turtle made a musical instrument with his friend's antlers. Every night, just before sunset, he would play it sitting on his doorstep. One of the people who happened to hear him playing was transfixed with delight. That was the ox called Butterfly, who was rambling toward the village for some important matter. The music was coming from the house of Turtle the recluse. Ox was perplexed, recalling that music used to enthrall him. He found himself face to face with Turtle, whose eyes were closed and whose spirit was obviously off in another world. Turtle held a strange, flaming instrument that was giving off the sublime sounds that so delighted Ox.

"In the name of all you hold dear, Turtle," said the ox, "give me your music."

Coming down from his unspeakably beautiful high, Turtle stared sadly at the enormous, exalted mass of the quadruped standing begging before him, and he thought in silence for a while.

"Give me your music, Turtle!"

"Alas, my friend. Your legs are too strong, and mine are too short. What happens if my music carries you off so far that, old and tired as I am, I can't keep up with you?"

"Don't insult me, Turtle. There are some things that we oxen just don't do."

"So you say. But anybody could yield to a bad urge. I can't grant you your wishes."

But Ox kept on begging Turtle to let him hear – just one more time – that divine "thing" that resonated in the instrument and made him, even him, tremble like a leaf, bringing tears to his eyes like the "Bogguará arayé" of midnight laments.

Eventually, Turtle gave in:

"Relax, my friend! I'll indulge you. But first, let me heat a little coffee."

And he set a pan full of tar on the fire.

"Here," he said, handing him the antlers. Strung with a string fine and blue like a vein, they were silent and lifeless. "With the heat from your hand and the power of your blood, the music will play itself."

Scarcely had the Ox touched them when he was flooded with music. He thought he was dancing among the stars. His body, usually a leaden weight, seemed like a feather. He felt like he was made of next to nothing, of something lighter and more sublime than the perfume on the breath of jasmine. His winged feet no longer touched the ground. He was soaring, the lightest and most graceful of creatures, and he was elated by such unexpected boundless bliss. And, like those who stop

45

in the midst of a dream's delights to make them last longer, he thought, "I sure won't give this back to Turtle for anything in the world!" And off he soared in his freedom dance, airy and free like the music that was etherizing him.

The tar was there boiling in its pot.

Then, out of his ethereal realm, suddenly Butterfly the ox fell to the ground, once again bitterly aware of his awful burdensome body. And his back was covered with black burning gunk. He fled as fast as he could, dragging his heavy body (with one less horn, "for a souvenir," said Turtle).

Another day, a heavyhearted scrawny horse was on his way to his fiancée's wake. As he passed by, he heard Turtle playing. Weeping and swearing that even if he were hungry, he would never steal the tiniest blade of grass, in a trance he also tried to run off with the music, for it made him whinny joyously, imagining himself in heaven's pastures. But then Turtle threw tar on his head, blinding him in one eye, and took some pruners and trimmed off one of his ears and the tail he used to chase flies away.

Just about every day, some animal would come and ask to borrow his instrument. Thanks to his ingenuity (the precious gift that was all his parents had left him), Turtle kept chopping off horns, tails, feet, ears, without over-extending himself (haste only leads to fatigue). He defended his wondrous music against people's widespread covetousness, which threatened to trap him at even the most unexpected times. And I'm not just talking about professional thieves like the magpie, but also about a respected matron like the sow, who commands everyone's respect and who can't be vain because she's so fat and busy with her sacred duties (she's only interested in her continual pregnancies and her enviable deliveries). One night she went to Turtle's, and trying hard not to be clumsy and be found out in the dark, she stole the sought-after object. If she hadn't grunted when she tripped over the doorway and fallen, Turtle never would have caught her red-handed.

Since he was dealing with a lady, Turtle didn't use the tar, which he always kept heating on the fire just in case. Instead, he thought it would be appropriate to strike her violently on her posterior, to which the matron objected loudly, her dignity bruised more than her opulent flesh.

"Oh! Mr. Turtle! Sir! A woman's backside is sacred. Whom do you take me for?"

Turtle's musical reputation spread throughout the province, though the people participating in those conversations never mentioned why they were missing some obvious part of their anatomy! Finally, Tiger, the master of us all, was going to celebrate his feast day nearby with a ball, a banquet, fireworks, and a speech in his honor, and he showed up one fine morning at Turtle's house. Turtle welcomed him with the utmost respect, for he was an Important Animal, claiming power and authority by his teeth. Turtle gave him the best of everything he had. He called for the six largest hens in his courtyard and had a huge basket of fruits and meats made ready for Tiger to take home to his family as a gift. Then the chief explained that he had come to invite Turtle to his party and to borrow his musical instrument, which, according to all the maimed people he had heard from, was by itself the equal of the best orchestras in the capital and in the entire civilized world.

"You're really too kind. This instrument, my most noble friend, is the comfort of my old age. I call it 'Cocorícamo,'[18] and I made it with my heart. It's been my only pleasure since I realized that my youth was gone. One fine day, you open your eyes and look within yourself and see that you're old. And

18. A Cabrera footnote explains Cocorícamo as "the imponderable."

women let you know it too, either with a disdainful look or by asking for money. Alas, boss, to lend is to lose, for as soon as you receive something you forget all about it. But enough of that! You're the master, the most honest, the most upright, the most carnivorous, the Savior of the Nation. And so the truth is, as much as it pains me to hand it over, I can't refuse your request to play 'Cocorícamo.'"

And while Tiger approved the truth of such well-deserved praises, Turtle placed the musical antlers he was holding in Tiger's hands.[19]

Grín! Grín! Grín!

Grín! Grín! Grín!

Grín! Grín! Grín!

Bongo Monasengo, Si kengó!

Bongo Monasengo, Si kengó!

Grín! Bongo Monasengo, Si kengó!

The music lifted Tiger forcefully from his stool, keeping him from answering. . . .

First a tickle – "grín! grín! grín!" – from the back of his neck all the way to his tail. Then the "Cocorícamo" generated such an intense pleasure, so painfully intense and continuous that he about went crazy and forgot how important he was. He twisted around, jumped in the air, wriggled, turned in circles, roared, lay on his back, and beat the air like an alley cat gone gaga, intoxicated by love and the moon. This powerful fellow who normally carried himself so majestically and powerfully was like a writhing tomcat making a fool of himself.

And then, instead of his imposing roar that could set the whole island quaking from one end to the other, he opened his mouth and his glorious throat let out an especially pa-

19. This sentence from the French version does not appear in the Spanish text.

thetic "meow." Turtle finished him off by dumping the pan of boiling tar on him. Tiger lay helpless in that fiery puddle of goo that was sticking to his skin and burning him all over. Then Turtle cut off nine of his toes and half his mustache and pulled out one of his canines. And, as if that weren't enough, he slapped him, calling him "faggot!" with each blow. Tiger went home in a sorry state, draped over his horse along with the basket and the six chickens who kept insulting him all the long way home, saying, "Fag, fag!"

Now his poor wife had just washed her hair that morning, and when she saw blood streaming from her husband, she collapsed in a faint into the arms of two slaves, and luckily they were good and strong. His daughters also managed to faint one after the other, until they realized that their father was still breathing. His sons, old enough already that they could avenge such an insult with one big bite of their teeth, asked him who was responsible for putting him in such a sorry state – injured, bleeding, sad, humbled, and without his mustache or his teeth. . . .

But no one could get him to break his determined silence, and he remained quiet throughout his slow recovery, wrapped in bandages and compresses made from spider webs and fresh scorpion oil.

It all kept eating away at him.

One word especially kept ringing in his ears:

"Faggot!"

Who knows? . . .

Five years went by. Five years, while Tiger examined his mutilated paws and secretly plotted his revenge.

For five years his good friend, his bosom buddy the rabbit, had been away on a trip. Then one fine morning, he showed up unexpectedly in the courtyard of the sugar mill.

"God must have sent you, Br'er Rabbit," said Tiger, embracing him warmly.

They spent the whole afternoon together, holed up in his room. He kept his voice low since walls have not only ears, eyes, and memory, but also a tongue, and a woman's viperous tongue at that. Tiger told Rabbit the truth about his nine shortened toes, the gap in his beautiful teeth that reminded everyone that he had lost a canine,[20] and the lumps and scars on his back – leaving out of course several less important details that were harder for him to accept than some of the others. Oh! Hadn't people already started calling him "the guy who's been clipped"? Now there's a word that really peeved him because of all the meanings it could suggest and because his enemies were slyly spreading it far and wide along with slanderous explanations that were damaging to his prestige and his authority.[21]

Rabbit grabbed a sack and a drum and headed out into the countryside.

Sandemania, sandemania!
Elúero kéngueré, kángara uirimakanga obbá . . .
Sandemania, sandemania!

Orders of the king,
calling all landowners to a meeting.

He beat his drum and proclaimed the royal edict standing on Cow's land, right next to Turtle's.

"If you see Turtle, Sister Cow, and can thus spare me the trouble of going to look for him, tell him to show up at the meeting."

---

20. The words "reminded everyone that he had lost a canine" can be found in the French version but not in the Spanish.

21. These last two sentences are not in the Spanish version.

He gave the same message to the donkey and the calico bull, who were neighboring farmers, and they wasted no time telling Turtle that the king had summoned him.

"He's probably raising taxes," grumbled Mrs. Cow, who quickly powdered her face and put on her canary-yellow satin shoes and her sky-blue muslin dress with embroidered flounces. Though sweaty and breathless, she was glad for the occasion to show off her earrings and her French gold necklace, and she set out for the village on her mule.

Some time later, Turtle heard the drum at his own gate.

"Are you still here, brother? A meeting has been called over in the village, and everyone is there but you and me."

"What meeting?" asked Turtle. "I heard something about it, but I wasn't paying attention."

"The king. He's called the meeting for right now. It's apparently a matter of some importance."

"I think I heard someone tell my good friend the cow that Tiger is presiding at the king's meeting."

"Br'er Turtle! You're imagining things. The Tiger? May he rest in peace in God's protection! He died more than two years ago. I myself was at his funeral, one of the finest around. A steeple fell on one of his paws, dew infected the wound, and gangrene claimed him in a matter of hours."

"What's this you're telling me, my man? First I've heard of that. We do live some distance apart, but I always respected him highly, and he deserved respect. Though it happened long ago, this news is hard for me. Gangrene of the foot? You must be kidding!"

"Well, nobody can escape death, not even a tiger."

"True enough. That's why people say that once when Death was hungry . . ."

"Hurry up, brother, let's not waste any more time. Put on

your hat and let's be off. You can tell me that story on the way. If you want, I can carry you in my basket."

"In your basket? I'd rather walk," thought Turtle. And he set off with Rabbit, a fine lad who was interesting to talk to. But after a while, Rabbit exclaimed:

"At this rate, we'll never get there! I could be there already, if you didn't drag your feet so much. Turtle, we've got to put you in my basket. I assure you that you don't weigh that much; I can run like a bullet."

"But it's not proper for me, a landowner, to show up at a meeting in a basket like a chicken!"

"I'll take you out when we near the village, and nobody will see anything."

So Turtle made himself comfortable in the basket, and Rabbit took off running.

"Are we about there?" he asked, raising the cover of the basket with his head, when he figured an hour had gone by.

"Still a long way to go."

(Sánsara, sánsara, sánsara.)[22] (Run, run, run.)

Another bumpy chaotic hour went by.

"Br'er Rabbit, I can't take much more of this sea-sickness. Can you see the village yet?"

"Still a ways to go."

(And sánsara, sánsara, sánsara.)

His stomach and his frozen guts hanging from his mouth, Turtle lifted the lid and asked once more:

"How much longer, brother?"

Finally, the motion stopped, along with the nausea and sea-sickness. . . . Turtle found himself face to face with Tiger and all his family.

"I think everyone's here now for the meeting!"

22. In Cabrera's dictionary, the word "sánsara" is said to mean "flee." In popular Cuban vernacular, it has come to mean "to walk."

And Turtle quickly pulled in his head, so he wouldn't have to watch his own death.

With crisp words, Tiger called for a banana plant to be brought.

"Show your face!" he roared. "Stick your head out! I'll smash it in, shell and all! See this banana plant? Get a good look at it, you scoundrel! I'm going to plant it myself, today, on St. Isidore's Day, the god of farmers. When it starts bearing and the fruit is ripe enough, I'll eat you with banana and okra stew. . . . Oh, and I'll drink your blood with *zambumbia*![23] But first, I sentence you to hunger and thirst for the rest of your life! So be it!"

He locked Turtle in a trunk and had him carried away unceremoniously to the loft.

Thoroughly satisfied, he then sat down to play a game of *tresillo*.[24] That very day, not only did he pardon some of his slaves who were being punished, but after lunch he also asked his wife to play "La Paloma" and "La Monona" on the piano, and he hadn't done that for five years![25]

Finally, when the banana plant had a nice stalk of bananas, Tiger went to buy a pot and invited his friend Rabbit, who held the lucrative positions of chief justice and fire chief, performing both with acknowledged skill. The little tigers took advantage of their father's absence by climbing into the loft. They opened the trunk just enough to see a dried-up, shriveled Turtle wasting away in a corner. The unpleasant screeching of the lock brought Turtle back to his senses, and he realized

23. *Zambumbia* is fermented cane juice with hot pepper.

24. *Tresillo* is a traditional game of cards.

25. "La Paloma" and "La Monona" are two traditional songs called *habaneras*. "La Paloma" was written by the Basque composer Sebastián Iradier Salaberri. The other may be an anonymous *habanera* in which the words "monona mía" are a part of the text.

that his last hour had come. But rather than waiting in anguish, he began to dance. That was the last thing the tigers expected, and they found it highly entertaining. The fresh air and the few rays of light that filtered into the chest after a year of total darkness revived Turtle a little.

One of the tigers, three minutes older than all the others, praised Turtle with all the touching spontaneity of youth:

"Bravo, Turtle! You can really dance!"

"Oh, your father is a better dancer than me!" he replied, his voice already distant and empty, like those who are dead long before they actually die.

"Ever since he single-handedly defeated a herd of elephants and fifty lions that had set upon him, Papa has limped a little."

"My dear children," sighed Turtle, suddenly brightening up and seizing on a moment of clarity, "if you put me in a basin of water, then you will see what real dancing looks like! . . . I'm not at my best when it's dry."

The tigers, their curiosity getting the better of them, tumbled down the stairs and came back as fast as they could with a basin filled to the brim with water.

Water! Blessed water! Just feeling it there, so close to his mouth, drinking in this wonderful liquid first with his eyes, Turtle's whole body came joyously back to life.

> "Pongueledió, el bongué![26]
> Pongueledió, el bongá!
> Pongueledió, el gongué!
> Pongueledió, el bongá!"

26. One possible interpretation for these words would be "start hitting the drums!" (from the infinitives "poner" and "dar" as well as different forms of the word "bongo").

And while the dazzled tigers watched, he danced a dance of thanks for the love of water and for his quenched thirst.

"Iebbé! Iebbé! Keep going, Turtle!" they shouted together from around the bowl, mesmerized by the rhythm."

"Oh, but in here I can barely move around," said Turtle. "If only we could find a stream!"

"Oh, yes! A stream! Let's find a stream!"

Once in the stream, Turtle just made a few awkward motions and sang:

> "Pongueledió, el bongué!
> Pongueledió, el bongá!
> Pongueledió, el gongué!
> Pongueledió, el bongá!"

"Children, it's really too bad there's not a river around here!"

Now the tigers could think of nothing else but dancing.

"Let's go to the river!"

There, in the broad current where he was free, Turtle danced so wildly that the tigers couldn't keep up with his frenetic pace. Instead of seeing only one Turtle, they stared confusedly at a thousand turtles.

"How about taking him to the sea?"

But now the eldest tiger, suddenly horrified and beginning to think that he was going to lose his head, said:

"God help us! It's already late. If Papa knew that we took Turtle out of the trunk, he'd give us a beating, like the day we smeared glue on his armchair."

And so he called out to the turtle:

"Turtle! That's enough. Come on out. Don't forget that we're eating you tonight in banana and gumbo stew."

"Oh, I'd nearly forgotten. I'm coming, my son," replied a thousand turtles, once again Turtle himself when he stopped moving. "But first, let me go down to the bottom to say good-bye to the river."

He found a stone about his size, rolled it in the mud along the bottom, shaped it to look just like him, and with his claws he carved marks just like the ones on his own shell, marks that nobody has ever been able to decipher. Then, stirring up the water, he pushed the stone gently toward the bank, where the tigers picked it up and ran back home with it.

When Tiger got back with his friend Rabbit and sacks full of food, he found the kids playing quietly on the front steps.

"An eye for an eye! A tooth for a tooth!" The friends went to the loft and opened the trunk. There was Turtle, just as they had left him a year before. His head was pulled in, out of shame and fear. He was in the same position, in the same hopeless corner. . . .

To make his presence known, and because he could no longer contain his anger, Tiger hit him with his machete . . . and the blade broke in half. . . .

"Man, pain really makes you tough!"

They subjected the turtle to a series of horrible, humiliating tortures.

But in the final analysis it was just a rock. Tiger couldn't squeeze even one drop of blood to drink in his *zambumbia* as he had sworn to do! Not a single strip of meat to flavor his banana and okra stew! Oh, well. . . . Anyhow, Turtle was there at the bottom of the pot and his suffering had to be excruciating! And on cue from Tiger, Rabbit felt it his duty to answer:

"Go ahead and eat him by yourself, brother. Your honor has been avenged."

Los Compadres

All of us are children of saints, and all of our meanness and the pleasure we take in sinning comes directly from them.

Following some run-ins with women, the most saintly saint of all had to flee Tácua country and ended up in the Ochún region. Changó was his name, or St. Bárbara, who also goes by Obakoso, Alafi, Agadgu,[1] Dádda, Obaiyé, and Lubbeo (Lubbeo being his given name).

A real Romeo, he was always itching to pick a fight and was the life of the party. The king of the earth, a braggart, but courageous nonetheless. Quite a handsome fellow, even if he was raised in the gutters. Wherever he was, along with his miracles, he would get himself into all sorts of trouble and have to race out of town. He spent his life running from town to town because many wanted to kill him, but he always got away.

In Ochún's country, *Lucumí* country, he fell in love with Ochún (the Virgin of Charity).[2] He made his conquest while dancing. She said "yes" immediately, and they began living together. Then one day, Ochún spoke to her older sister Yemayá, Our Lady of Regla, and said:

"If you could see the black fellow I have, you'd be crazy jealous."

"What fellow?" Yemayá asked.

Changó was always with an old man, a shadow of his shadow who looked after him, and the old man had already said to Yemayá:

The father and the godfather of a child are considered to be *compadres*.

1. The name Agadgu can be found only in the French version.

2. Ochún is also called La Caridad del Cobre.

57

"When you meet Changó, call him Lubbeo. He's your son."

Yemayá insisted on seeing Changó. And Changó seduced Yemayá, and Yemayá was pleased to be seduced. But just as they were about to make love, Yemayá suddenly remembered and shouted out:

"Lubbeo, you are my son!"

And she gave him milk from her breast.

The news shocked Ochún so much that her head almost fell off. She grabbed her head and put it back in place, saying:

"My nephew! He was my nephew!"

Yes, but it was too late. There was nothing to be done.

Dolé wasn't really a bad girl. She was Ochún's daughter. She wasn't allowed to eat squash, partly because squash contains Ochún's secret but mostly because of what had happened in the well.

And here is what had happened. Yemayá, while she was Orula's (St. Francis of Assisi's) wife, didn't trust Ochún. Orula lived in a well, and Ochún would slip down into it.

Yemayá started spying, and she saw Ochún sneaking down into the well. Quietly, she tiptoed off to find the Supreme Being under his shelter.

"Babamí! Come and see something, Babamí!"

The Supreme Being, who rules over all of them, Cholá, and Orichaoko, and Olua, Oyá, Oloku, Ogba, Ogún, Ochosí, Babaluayé, Obaoddé, Sodgi, Nanú, Nanáburukú, Obatalá, as well as the Ibeyis and the Elegguás.[3] Babamí is older than

3. The name Olua is in only the French version. Oyá is a female Yoruba goddess who often accompanies Changó; she is an *orisha* of change and new beginnings. The mother of the Ibeyi, the divine twins, and also of Elegguá, she is sometimes identified as the Virgin of Candelaria. Nanú is the mother of Babalúayé. Nanáburukú is the grandmother of Babalúayé.

time, and he has more power than everyone else, just as Changó has more power than all the saints.

Yemayá leans out over the well, tugging at Babamí's sleeve: "Papa! Kuanchaca okó con okó!"

And she points her finger to show the Supreme Being what Ochún and Orula are doing in their secret hiding place.

"Very well then," said the Everlasting Father. "Let St. Francis stay forever with Charity (Orula with Ochún)!"

Dolé wasn't evil, but she wasn't very faithful either. All the men lusted after her, but the man who pleased her the least was her husband, a freed slave who rolled cigars for a living. He had lived most of his life in the country and wasn't as cunning[4] as the city blacks.

Dolé's lover was with her in the bedroom when her husband came in unexpectedly from the street. She hid the man under the bed, then went and opened the door with her hair messed up and looking distraught and tearful. (There's no woman who's not adept at lying.)[5]

"Oh, how it hurts! Oh, my stomach! Oh, Evaristo! If you don't run to get some cure from the doctor priest,[6] I'm done for. Evaristo, I'll breathe my last gasp, I swear."

And then she threw herself on to the bed, writhing in pain and biting the pillow.

"Your stomach hurts? What are you talking about? What cure? What doctor?" wondered Evaristo. (Evaristo de la Torre de Cienfuegos was his true illustrious name.) Dolé, in spite of

4. In the French version, instead of "cunning" it says "speaking Spanish," which was a sign of the city dweller's craftiness.

5. This parenthetical information is not in the French edition.

6. In Spanish, "doctor priest" is *el brujo*, another word for the *babalao*, who combines the functions of herb doctor, priest, spiritual adviser, and medium.

her pain, explained as best she could how that morning when he had gone off to work and she had begun to do the house-work, she had felt a stabbing pain high in her stomach. The pain was so intense that after it had subsided a little, she had gone to see the local *brujo*. He had questioned her and then told her, on behalf of Oyá, that it was serious. There was some animal in her stomach, a twisted, hairy monster, toad, spider, sponge, or crab, with teeth as sharp as pins. She could get rid of it only by eating a fresh alligator egg. There was nothing but an alligator egg that could calm the ravenous hunger of that vicious beast, which otherwise would finish her off by chewing her entrails.

"It really hurts! The creature is tearing into me with his teeth! Do you realize, Evaristo, what is happening in my guts?"

Poor Evaristo was a good fellow, and he dearly loved his little wife, so he was filled with pity at the thought of her guts being eaten up. So he rushed off to the river to find an alliga-tor egg.

Then Dolé's lover could come back out. He was all sweaty and bruised, and they had a good laugh at the expense of the poor idiot who might even get swallowed by an alligator.

> "Saúla bómbo, saúla bómbodil,
> Saúla bómbo, saúla! The idiot is gone!"

The female alligator had laid four eggs. But she had posted a guard to watch them, and she herself never strayed far when looking for food. Whenever she heard the slightest noise – a dislodged pebble, some rustling in the reeds, a step – she would rush to the defense of her eggs. Evaristo had to run for his life.

He went back many times to the river to try to steal the

alligator's eggs, and Dolé, having nothing to fear, giggled and dallied with her deary.[7]

> "Saúla bómbo, saúla bómbodil!
> Saúla bómbo, saúla! The idiot left!"

Right across from their house lived Evaristo's *compadre*, Capinche the stevedore. He lived with an attractive washerwoman who was also a *santera*, and it was said that when she went into her trance she would eat fire just like Yánsa.[8] Evaristo had been the godfather of a little girl that Capinche had had with another woman, Maria Virtudes. In the evening, they would go to the general store to play dominoes. In earlier days, they had cut a lot of cane together. Now they were both free. Evaristo rolled cigars at the factory, and Capinche carried loads on the wharves and had slowly become knock-kneed.

Capinche had trouble swallowing that story about alligator eggs and about painful gnawings in her stomach because he and his washerwoman had seen the other fellow come and go many times, and not just when Evaristo went to the river.

"Well then, no egg?" asked Dolé feebly when her husband returned panting, his pants dripping with mud and his hands empty.

"Any closer and the alligator guard would have had me by the foot!"

"Ah, dear God! Mother! Now I'll never get well," moaned Dolé. "Though I am feeling a little better now. Perhaps the critter is taking a nap. It's not chewing at me anymore."

---

7. "Deary" is a translation for "Su 'alé'," identified in an author's note as *amante*.

8. *Santera* means priestess. "She would eat fire" is the translation of "Se comía la 'mangoma.'" (*Mangoma* is identified in an author's note as *candela*.)

The animal indeed seemed to be sleeping and wasn't hurting her now. He was sleeping like a baby. Dolé could get up and move around, and she could work as if she were in perfect health.

One day, Evaristo's *compadre* had drunk a little too much and said to him:

"You sure are an idiot, old buddy! A first-class idiot, no offense intended! Your woman has nothing wrong with her stomach. What she has on her mind is fooling around, and when she gets those feelings there's a big black stud hidden under her bed who gobbles up your goodies while you're beating your brains out working."[9]

Evaristo gave no answer. He gritted his teeth, and without even saying good-bye he went home. Dolé was already half asleep. Evaristo maybe felt like strangling her, but he wasn't a hothead. To be sure, he had killed a salt-water Negro several years earlier, a Ñanigo fellow named Rufino, but he had done it by accident, had just hit him too hard.[10] And nobody had ever found out. And also one time he had stabbed a fellow during a hot argument at carnival time. But only because the dance and cheap alcohol had excited him, not at all because he meant evil.[11] And nobody had suspected anything that time either. And when people don't think you're a bad guy, you're a good guy.

9. "Big black stud" is a translation of the Spanish text's *un negro chévere*.

10. A salt-water Negro is a translation of the Spanish text's *un congo*. The word Ñánigo can refer to special secret language spoken by members of special all-male African associations (*abakuás*) and presumably to those who are members of those associations. The word also refers to certain ancestral spirits.

11. "Cheap alcohol" is a translation of *malafo*, identified by the author as cane alcohol. The word is probably African in origin, for in some Bantu languages, including Kikongo, the word for liquor or wine is *malafu*.

He tore off his coat and his pants, making a real mess of the room. His shoes crashed against the wall, and in his choked-up voice he said to Dolé:

"Where is that nasty critter, where is it?"

"Shhh," she answered as she woke up.

Evaristo looked under the bed. He opened the armoire. Compadre Capinche must just be drunk – it was Saturday after all. Just the thoughts of a drunk and maybe just some mean gossip, and from a good friend too. He himself had never seen anyone sneaking around his house. So now he was scared that Dolé's critter might wake up again with its craving for an egg. He pulled the sheet up over his head, leaving his feet sticking out (and it's not wise to let your bare feet stick out from under the sheet, because errant souls from purgatory could come and grab them with their cold hands). And then he fell asleep, snoring away as he did every night.

A few days later Dolé's pain came back, worse than ever. This time, the same animal was itself shouting, welling up in the woman's throat and scolding the poor husband directly:

"Come on, you jerk, you coward! Go get me an alligator egg. I'm tired of waiting. Otherwise, I'll gobble her up, and it'll be your fault. And then, I'll get inside you too and eat you up as well!"

That made a real impression on Evaristo, and he set out at once, swearing that even if it meant leaving half his body in the river, he'd come back with the cure.

As he was rounding a street corner, he had a worrisome thought.

"The truth comes out of the mouths of drunks and children. My friend was totally drunk. What if he's right?"

And with that he stopped short, wondering what to do. A neighbor woman opened her shutters and shouted out to him in mockery:

"Looking for another alligator egg, my dear man?"

"May God protect you, old boy," said the Galician shop-keeper who was playing dominoes at his counter with his black clients. He stood there in his shirtsleeves, his open shirt showing his white hairy chest. As he serves a mulatto woman a few cents' worth of wine in an old olive can, he laughingly whispers something to her through his Spanish-style up-turned mustache. She looks Evaristo up and down and then twists her mouth in sympathy.

Evaristo then runs into Mateo, the chicken man.

"Chickens! Fat chickens! Cheap!"

"Good morning, Mateo."

"Have you already stolen an egg from Mama Alligator?" asked Mateo with obvious delight.

Everyone is watching. Making fun of him!

"You're a first-class idiot!" repeats his friend, now no longer drunk but perfectly clearheaded.

Evaristo goes back home, smashes the door down with one blow. And sure enough, there's Dolé, being all lovey-dovey and familiar with some man.

What really makes Evaristo angry, and rightly so, is seeing the fellow's clothes on the coat hook and seeing him lying in his very bed, in the hollow his very own body had formed in the mattress. And by God! The man's head on his very own pillow! He grabs the first thing he can find, a bottle, and breaks it over the intruder's head. Then he falls upon him like a crazed animal, biting him, kicking him, even butting him with his head.

"But we weren't doing anything bad!" swore Dolé brazenly. "We were just chatting! He's one of my country cousins, and he was so tired."

The fellow managed to escape into the street, stark naked. Some women screeched:

"Catch him! Catch him!"

And there the Galician shopkeeper grabbed him for Evaristo, with the aid of two other neighbors and the chicken man, who was still holding a cluster of lively chickens in his right hand and the man with his left. The whole neighborhood knew that something like this would happen sooner or later. Nobody was surprised by the turn of events.

"Police, police! Nobody move!"

The civil guard had caught a whiff of something. The fellow standing with no shirt on his back, and Dolé gesticulating and rambling on, unable to stop! The crowd of curious onlookers got quiet and waited expectantly.

"A simple argument, Mister Law and Order! Yes, that's all. But now it's over. And nothing at all happened."

The policemen brandished their sticks impressively. They scowled through their black, bushy eyebrows (one had no space at all between his eyebrows). There they stood, symbols of justice, there on the sidewalk, leaning against one of those big bay windows low to the ground. They stood twisting their mustaches menacingly, for they always have it in for black people.

In all the commotion, the mulatto customer's wine had splashed out on the ground. She walked off lugging her empty can and mumbling to herself about wasting all that good wine. A few of the women hurried over to Dolé to give her some herbal tea. Evaristo couldn't bear to raise his head. They had made a real fool of him! His friends slapped him on the back to make him feel better.

"Oh, if only the police hadn't shown up, that jerk wouldn't have been long for this world!"

Finally the policemen move off, prancing haughtily in their boots.

That evening the whole neighborhood shows up at Evaristo's house in case he should try to do something stupid. It's as if there's a party at his house, or a wake, which is about the same thing. Even passing strangers give their opinion when they stop to look in through the open door and are told the details of the situation. Each neighbor brings something to help pass the time at the wake: a chunk of cheese, guava paste, some crackers, some coffee, a tin of sardines, some beer, or some cheap alcohol.[12]

"We must certainly not leave Evaristo and Dolé alone just now!"

"Don't do anything you'll regret," advises the *santera* laundry woman.

Surrounded by his male friends, there's Evaristo, seated on a trunk sidesaddle. He is still furious, and doggedly keeps muttering the same obscenity. Dolé, sitting in an armchair, still only partially clothed, sighs again and again. Her voice is broken by sobs; she raises her arms and then lets them drop. Her head is aching, she says. "My skull is exploding!" The women standing near her take turns fanning her, but there's no way to loosen the iron band she feels around her neck. They put more herb tea on the stove to boil.[13]

Finally Evaristo's *compadre* arrives, his best friend Capinche, whom everyone has been waiting for. He goes straight to the heart of things with all the authority that being Evaristo's *compadre* gives him.

"Evaristo, what's this I hear? We must set an example of good upbringing. Everything's over. For us, it's ancient history. And indeed, you've acted like a true gentleman."

"No," Evaristo answers. "It's not over. Dolé should never have done what she did to me without my consent!"

12. In the French version, the word *chichipo* is used instead of alcohol and is glossed as "limonade gazeuse" (soda water).

13. This sentence is found only in the French version.

"Oh, my dear man!" exclaims Dolé, weeping hot tears. "If you want me to go away, I'll be off. But I'd rather you killed me, my love, my angel! Because you are the man I love, my treasure, my dear! You're the man I love!"

"Sure. Well, if I ever find you in bed again with someone else, I'll smash you into baby food, I will!"

"Never again, Evaristo!"

Capinche had permission from the authorities to organize some drumming. So some drummer friends of the couple showed up, plus Dolé's goddaughter, who was six months pregnant and who had hurried over when she heard what was happening.

Evaristo's anger slowly faded away.

By three in the morning, everyone was dancing.

From the back room of his store, the Galician shopkeeper could hear the drum booming. With all the bursts of laughter and the noise that his black neighbors were making, plus the heat, the mosquitoes, and the bedbugs that had faithfully followed him from Spain, he couldn't get to sleep.

"Oh, brother! These blacks! They think that dancing can take care of everything. They dance when they're born, they dance when they die, they dance for killings. They have to celebrate everything, even the horns their wives make them grow!"

The black *santera* washerwoman who lived with Capinche died from a bad cold. Or more likely from a certain procedure that the *mayombero*[14] did for her. Nobody dies a natural death. And she had some enemies among those with magical powers. Some were powerful enemies. When she was told that somebody had heard her name spoken "over the cauldron,"

14. A *mayombero* is a priest from the *palo mayombe* religion practiced in Cuba by some descendants of slaves from the Congo region.

the spell was already pretty far along, and the talisman made to protect her didn't do any good at all. Somebody had worked too fast. That's what black magic is – continuous hidden warfare. A nail can protect you from another nail, but if a spell is cast properly by a sorcerer[15] who knows his stuff, it is very difficult to escape it. And so the poor woman said as she died:

"Not even Santa Bárbara is of any help to me now. Nor is my new talisman."

And she left this world, leaving Capinche a little black three-year-old with crooked legs like him, whom Dolé and Evaristo carried to be baptized. And since Evaristo was the boy's godfather, he and Capinche were doubly linked by the sacraments and doubly *compadres*. The little fellow grew up in Dolé's house, and Capinche would spend his free moments in his friend's quarters.

Dolé had a sewing machine now. Tobacco had finally gotten to Evaristo's lungs, and he would often wake up coughing blood. So on such days, it felt like he hadn't a drop of blood left in his veins, and he couldn't go to work. Dolé had become a seamstress to help him earn some money, for she wasn't a bad sort at all. She had a big heart. The saints, according to the consultation[16] that was arranged for Evaristo, kept asking for goats, pigeons, roosters to be sacrificed and ordered him to eat a lot of raw meat and to drink lots of eggnog. The pharmacist tried to heal him with a very expensive French prescription. One *centén!*[17] That's what the medicine cost, and it wouldn't last any time at all!

Capinche also contributed to the household budget. He gave everything he made, absolutely everything. So thanks to him, his *compadre* could afford the patent medicine. But Cap-

15. In Spanish, "sorcerer" is *un brujo.*
16. A consultation is "*un sarayeyéo.*"
17. A *centén* was a gold coin worth five pesos in Cuba.

inche no longer had a woman in his own house and went out with a different woman every night, and sometimes he didn't have any woman at all. He began to be taken with Dolé. And then he fell in love for good. One day, he didn't leave for work at the docks. She was alone, working at her sewing machine. Capinche sat down beside her. He watched her silently, his nostrils dilating.

Suddenly, he grabbed her in his arms, saying:

> "My comadre,[18] my comadre,
> How I love her.
> Let's go make love, my girl!"

Dolé pushed him away and crossed herself. To tell the truth, she didn't find him unappealing. And indeed she might really have enjoyed . . . But what about the sacrament of baptism? The *sacrament*! And there the two stood, trembling with embarrassment.

"Ah, Dolé, Dolé, why the sacrament?"

"God only knows!"

Now a pig before being a pig looked very much like a man. It was a man. He offended his mother, and she put a curse on him. So he became a pig, with four feet, a fat tummy, a snout for digging, and a corkscrew tail. But inside, he is just like a man.

A *compadre* who betrays his *compadre* after they've been tied together by the body of Christ risks uncounted calamities. The punishment is horrible. A woman who conducts herself badly with her *comadre* – or with her *compadre*, which would be the same thing – is digging her own grave, and she can even picture the worms eating her. Her soul would need masses said for centuries.

18. Comadre appears in the Spanish as *mi cumari*.

That's what happened to Cecilia Alvarado, from Arroyo Naranjo.[19] She lay in agony fully conscious for twenty-two days because she had betrayed her *comadre*. (She had spent money her *comadre* had entrusted to her and then had said horrible things about her to justify herself.) The family council gathered and agreed to persuade the offended woman to forgive her. In spite of what she knew, she did forgive her, and the poor woman could finally turn toward the wall and die in peace. But if she hadn't been pardoned, what would have awaited her under the earth?

So you can't take sacraments or the saints lightly. One of Evaristo's friends had been run over by a cart full of mangoes. And why? Because he had promised he would build an altar to St. Lazarus, to Babalúayé, if he won the lottery. He won a lot of money, rented a fruit shop, bought himself a horse and a cart, and spent the rest having a good time, completely forgetting his promise to build an altar to St. Lazarus. Then St. Lazarus, through a shell reading, had some messages sent to him:

"How about my altar? Do you think I'm a kid, playing me for a fool like that? If you don't take care of what you promised me, get ready to die a horrible death."

But the man acted like a smarty-pants, and answered lightly:

"Oh, the old fellow can wait. He's in no hurry."

Well, one day when he was walking along, he was run over by another fruit merchant's cart, nobody knows just how.

How unfortunate to be *compadres*, linked by the sacraments! How vexing for Dolé and Capinche! They were in love, but they didn't dare act. Capinche would show up at times when Evaristo wasn't around.

"Ah, my *comadre*, how I love her.
Let's go make love, my *comadre*."

19. Arroyo Naranjo is a town in Havana Province.

Such was his refrain. And it was tough for Dolé to resist. But fear was stronger, and she couldn't forget the sacrament. Capinche would lower his eyes, bite his lips until they bled, and walk off cursing under his breath.

One day while she was struggling to get loose from Capinche's grasp, he said to her:

"Evaristo is thin as a rail. You can see death in his face."

"When he's dead, Capinche, then, yes," she answered. "Wait until he's dead!"

Capinche thought:

"Since my pal is about to die, it wouldn't matter if he died a little early. He wouldn't suffer as long."

Poor Evaristo soon was barely able to sit up in bed without help. Nonetheless, his eyes would brighten with hope when Dolé came back from the butcher shop and proudly held up chunks of blood-red meat. But they were too much for him to eat, and when he finally was unable to eat anything at all anymore, he still put his faith in the spoonfuls of the prescription that was surely infallible since it was so expensive. He would ask for some of it at all hours of the day and painfully swallow it with fervor. But there came a day when there was no money to buy it with, and Capinche, instead of giving him some of the saving syrup of liquid gold, suggested giving him a special herb brew[20] made by a black *santero*.

As evening fell, the poor fellow began to gasp for breath. He coughed one last time, a little dry wool-like cough. The sheets felt uncomfortable, and so did his restless hands. He wanted to see light, the great morning light that belongs to healthy men. He spoke of getting up, saying that he would go walking in the country, on the sugar mill property where he had been born. There in the slave quarters, he could hear his

---

20. "Special herb brew" appears in the Spanish as *unas yerbas de negrería*.

mother calling him. Why did she want to see him? All his dead relatives were calling him too. Later, he relaxed and dozed off. He must have died like a little bird, for Dolé never noticed that he made the slightest sound. She went and lit an oil lamp and came over to give him a cup of milk.

"Oh, good God! Evaristo is dead. He has gone out like a candle, the poor fellow! He didn't want to bother anyone, even to kick the bucket! That's just like him! Patient, quiet, calm, even when he dies. Oh, Blessed Mother! After so much effort, so much steak, so many prayers, so many one-*centén* prescriptions! When his *compadre* hears the news!"

People went to the docks to tell him the news.

"Please forgive us for what we have to say, but your *compadre* is dead."

Capinche paid all the funeral costs. What wouldn't one do for a *compadre*! When you've drunk so many of the good things of life with him, you have to accept the bitter as well. He mourned him with such pain that seeing him like that could have broken anyone's heart.

"Capinche, men don't cry!"

And he wiped his tears with a red kerchief that had belonged to his dead friend.

Who would have thought that so quickly . . . such a fine fellow as Evaristo was . . . Everyone in the neighborhood respected him. Never a misplaced word. Always ready to lend a hand!

They praised his virtues, his good sense, his urbanity. Especially his urbanity, now that most blacks had become such vulgar riff-raff! For raising their kids right, so they would be respectful, there was nobody like the people who came directly from Africa. Creoles, and children of Creoles, couldn't be conducting themselves worse. What a difference there was between them and good old African stock like Evaristo!

Dolé, in despair, would no sooner finish one crying spell than she would start another.

There lay Evaristo between four candles that were also crying. Now people could see how thin he had become. He was nothing but skin and bones. However . . .

"How fine he looks! And how lifelike!"

All the blacks of Congo Real, his *cabildo*,[21] showed up, circumspect and ceremonious. Others came from Pueblo Nuevo, from Santa Bárbara. There were friends from the cigar factory, the stevedores who worked with Capinche, friends of friends, distant acquaintances of the dead man, or of no one in particular.

"Our hearts are with you!"

"Our hearts with you!"

All the neighbors brought their chairs. They sit down, elbow to elbow, around the corpse. The kitchen's a mess, but they've set up a camp cot there in case some women collapse during the night and need to lie down somewhere.

Dolé comes into the room unsteadily, as if she were walking in her sleep. She wakes up and bursts out:

"Oh, my Evaristo!" she says to the corpse. "Open your eyes, my angel, and look at your Dolé. Look at your *compadre*. Look at your godson José. Look at all your friends who are here."

Her voice rises:

"Oh, my God! My God! Why have you taken him from me, my God? This morning he woke up so full of life and so frisky. He wanted to go out walking, and now he can't even speak anymore! He can't say 'Dolé' anymore! Oh my, oh my. Why have you left me, my man? He paid for my room, the dear man

21. The *cabildos* were Afro-Cuban societies of mutual aid, organized according to the African origins of the members. In 1755 there were twenty-one *cabildos* in Havana.

who loved me. Oh my, my dear man who was better than good bread! My dear black man! My husband, it's all over!"

She embraces the corpse, shaking it like a plum tree.[22]

"We've got to get her away from the corpse, so she can't see it anymore! The poor thing! She's inconsolable. It's as if she's completely crazed, but that's not surprising."

And all the women begin to shout like Dolé, each louder than the other. Two or three stiffen and fall heavily to the floor, as if on cue. Then they begin to convulse and froth at the mouth.

One old man, a salt-water Negro[23] who was pleased with such an outpouring of grief that made it a good wake, said to Dolé:

"Moana,[24] we will now pray for the corpse."

THE CHORUS: Let us now *langaína, ainganso!*

　　Let us now *langaína, ainganso* . . .

DOLÉ: He died!

THE CHORUS: Let us now *langaína, ainganso!*

DOLÉ: Do you remember?

THE CHORUS: Let us now *langaína, ainganso!*

　　Let us now *langaína, ainganso* . . .

DOLÉ:Alas, dear God! What pain!

Until late in the night, they exchanged stories about wakes. After all, they had to entertain their friends and the dead man until morning. One Creole man told about the wake held for a local black man, a pure African, over yonder on a coffee plantation near Pinar del Río.[25]

"He was a dark-skinned cowherd who was very old when

22. The phrase "like a plum tree" is found only in the French version.

23. "Salt-water Negro" appears as *un bangoche* in the French.

24. *Moana* means "woman."

25. Pinar del Río is the westernmost Cuban province.

he died. They wrapped him naked in a sheet and laid him out in a corner of his hut. For candles, they used earthenware bottles. They painted his face with plaster. By eight o'clock in the evening, all the black plantation workers had so filled up the hut that you couldn't have slipped a needle between them. Around eleven, they made up a song to sing all night and enjoy themselves for a while according to the tradition: 'You sit over here, I'll sit over there.' And the fellow who led with his drum and who was chanting the couplet had put on his jacket. And here's how they began to sing:

'Dreaming *cabobolla*, dreaming *cabobolla*, dreaming *cabobolla, reketetén, quereketén!*'

And with those words, the dead man sat up, moving as if he were rowing a canoe.

'Well, there's a fellow who is rising up to drum dance too.'

And sure enough, the dead man began to dance, a white handkerchief holding his jaws shut. And he banged three times on the drum, just as if he were alive! In terror, the Creole blacks ran away. But not the Africans! They kept on dancing with the dead man, yes, that's how they used to do things, until the fellow wrapped himself back up in his shroud and lay there all stiff and serious waiting for them to carry him off on his litter."

"That goes to show that with a drum you can wake up the dead," said Capinche sagely.

At five, in the first light of dawn, they carried off Evaristo in the white wood casket painted black that his *compadre* had paid for.[26] Impertinent flies were already buzzing about. And the corpse was beginning to smell. Then once again people began to fall apart and burst into tears. Dolé swore she would

26. The words "they carried off . . . had paid for" are found only in the French version.

75

soak her clothes in alcohol and strike a match if they carried him off.

"It's a pleasure to see how she mourns her dead husband! We couldn't ask her to do anything else!"

They called Capinche over to console her. Then they put the lid on the black pine casket, and it didn't fit very well. Since Capinche was Evaristo's best friend, when the time came to say good-bye, he measured himself with a string and threw the string in the casket. That way the dead man, thinking he was taking his friend with him, wouldn't have any reason to come after him or play tricks on him. The women stayed all day long weeping with Dolé and pitying her. Then the ceremonies for the dead continued.

But, that Evaristo – oh! May he rest in peace![27] – who had been such a well-behaved fellow, as soon as the soil had been thrown over him, with the sound of the wind blowing through the pines in the cemetery, the very first night, dark and troubled, Evaristo sets out in search of his home.

And there he discovers Capinche and Dolé. Capinche has his hands on Dolé's hips and is saying:

> "Oh, my *comadre*, my *comadre*. How I love her,
> Let's make love, my *comadre*."

But Dolé refuses, saying:

"Not yet, Capinche! We've just buried him. Wait a few days more. We must be careful."

The dead man's soul – who always ends up finding out about how the living have betrayed him – became angry, nasty, and vindictive. And so his soul said to them:

"That's a fine way to show how you feel about me! And he's the *compadre* I was sure of! And I've scarcely begun to rot."

27. "May he rest in peace" is a translation of *Requiéncantinpáche* (*requiem in pace*).

Dolé hears some unexplainable noises. And sometimes when she's alone, she hears some muffled steps in the room. Taps on the woodwork, like fingers drumming. And on the door, on the table, on the doorjambs, louder still. She can count them – one, two, three – but they are so fast and happen so frequently that she can't keep them straight. The robe hanging on its nail sways, although everything is shut tight as a sign of mourning, and no air is stirring. A sleeve rises up, as if an arm were in it. The bed frame creaks with someone else's weight as she is getting ready for bed. She wraps up in a sheet, but someone pulls it off of her. Someone whispers in her ear. Imperceptibly, as if trying not to be noticed, Evaristo's armchair rocks back and forth. After the candle has burned out and everything is pitch black, the darkness deepens and moves. In the room, night breathes painfully. Nothing can sleep.

Something shakes her bed, and fingernails drum on the foot of her bed. At the sound, she can recognize the cigar roller's long fingernails. The sewing machine starts up for a moment, as if something has fallen in its guts; a lock grates; and the closet door opens with a long screech. In truth, there is no way to get any rest in that bedroom. When Dolé wakes up, she is worn out. The room is already bathed in sunshine reflected by the white walls. It seems like someone has intentionally moved the wobbly table that has an old sock under one leg to stabilize it. The broken-handled jug that was keeping some watercress fresh, the bottle of rancid oil, two plates and a highfalutin butter dish and a half-empty sugar bowl, all fall to the ground with a deafening crash. Dolé, even when she's alone, knows that she's not really alone. She is forever turning around suddenly because she has felt a tenacious presence behind her. She never sees anything specific, but she senses things. She can hear perfectly well that someone is calling her: "Dolé!"

In the middle of the wall, Evaristo's picture that he admired so much is hanging at a steep angle. (Dolé straightens it with the greatest respect.) It's a charcoal drawing of Evaristo with a starched collar, a gold chain, and a tie, a very black tie, as if he were engraved on smoke. It looks like a portrait from the Spiritist Center, and he already looked like a dead man, even when he was alive. It frightens Dolé to death. But Capinche continues to pester her. He's getting demanding and tries to force her to keep her promise!

"When the snake is dead, so is its poison," he says.[28] "Once the dead man is buried, the living can have fun."

As Dolé takes her clothes off, her eyes catch sight of the picture:

"In the name of your mother," she blubbers, "don't go any further. Look at Evaristo! With his spittoon and his shiny watch. It's just as if he were here. How do you think we can enjoy each other like that?"

They couldn't, of course. One day passed, then another. All because of that damned portrait.

One day Capinche was coming back from the docks with a jar of coconut jam for Dolé when he found a flock of women at his doorstep and inside the house. They were whispering, gesticulating, and moving around the house. One was washing a cup, another, half-suffocating, was wrapping up Dolé who was shivering with cold in her bed and moaning in agony. Another went to the window and asked those gathered on the sidewalk to go get a mustard plaster and borrow two or three more blankets.

28. In Spanish the text says, "Se acabó el perro, se acabó la rabia." (In French, "morte la bête, mort le venin.")

"They asked me to go find you like the other time," said a mulatto stepping out of Capinche's way, "but I couldn't."

Dolé had complained of coldness moving in waves toward her heart. She had asked a neighbor for help. They could hardly understand her. She was barely mumbling and collapsed in the helping arms of her friends. All they could grasp was that she was going to die, "that death was freezing her." After several convulsions during which she seemed to be struggling desperately, she had fallen into a state of absolute lethargy. It was as if her five senses as well as her mind had been frozen solid.

They tried to speak to her:

"Dolé, come on, tell us what the matter is, dear woman."

But she wouldn't answer. All she could do was shiver and let her teeth chatter, and from time to time her eyes would open wide as if she were looking for something or asking anxiously for what she needed. But what it was, nobody could guess.

They had piled seven blankets on her. All the blankets they could find in the neighborhood, but even they couldn't keep her warm. The neighbor, rubbing her legs with a brush, then massaging her and covering her back up, said that the coldness she felt must be from death itself. Then the dying woman recognized Capinche for a second. Her eyes, like two shooting stars, were staring at Evaristo's portrait. Suddenly, Evaristo's eyes went blank. And everyone present shrank back in terror. They realized that the dead man had come to get her, and that he was carrying her off. Dolé's heart had frozen in its ice. There was nothing to be done.

"To save her, what didn't we try? Tell me. Dolé was trying to die, trying to die! And sure enough, Dolé has died. She has slipped right through our fingers."

And they all rubbed themselves to get warm again.

In less than a week, Capinche had lost two *compadres*. Misfortune was raining down on his head.

He didn't cry. But he chewed his fists, raging at death and losing all control.

"Come now, console yourself," they said to him. But he kept roaring back his answer, "NO!" Even if the Just Judge, the white God himself with his sideburns and his blue gown had come to him saying: "Listen, Capinche, I'm the one who gives life. And so I'm the one who takes it away at my pleasure. And that's how I want it." The Just Judge would throw him down, rip off his beard, and would break his ribs with his orangutan feet. Just let them come, Santa Bárbara with her Kumabondo club, and Ogbá with his sword, and Oyá with a lightning bolt, and all the other black saints! All the saints, like the white God, who throw stones but then pretend it wasn't them. (Capinche cursed and swore.) They never show their true colors. They just enjoy playing with men like a cat with a mouse. Abusing their power.

They laid out Dolé at the very place they had laid out Evaristo . . . rolling the bed into the middle of the bedroom.

The same people who had been at Evaristo's wake came to hers as well. But they were all sad and withdrawn, sitting in silence! A silent wake, a sad one, lacking its normal activity, with all the people reflecting seriously on death, which could with no apparent motive strike anybody at any time, even the strongest among them. That's the life we long for, my friends! No guarantees! Like a dream. And just on loan to us. The ancient newness of their discovery left them exhausted. Furthermore, with this particular death, there was something else. It wasn't a death like all the others. No sirree! Everyone, in the darkness of their souls, was so aware of the situation that nobody dared even talk about it. And there all the time was Evaristo's portrait, more ashen, more distant, really nothing more than a tie. But it was enough to dominate the gathering of blacks. His presence was felt more strongly than it had ever been felt, even when he was alive!

"Watch out, Capinche has gone dangerously mad," an old woman whose head was covered with a mantilla suddenly shouted. "Something bad is going to happen. José María, let me out of here!"

And that's what happened, nothing more, nothing less. Nobody will ever be able to forget it all.

When the old woman, panic-stricken, was shouting "Capinche has gone mad!," Capinche, wheezing like an ox, was dragging himself over to the dead woman's feet.

"Don't make such a fuss," grunted the other old man, José María, to calm her down. Go ahead and weep quietly. Nobody goes crazy because his *comadre* has died. He just goes about finding another one."

"I'm leaving, because I don't want to witness what's going to happen. You'll see. You know full well that the 'saints' are really like a storm about to burst over our heads."

Capinche was acting like an animal, a beast from hell. That's how they saw him. He kept speaking to the dead woman and to the others. Everyone rose as if on cue, and stood waiting. . . .

Capinche:

> "Dolé won't answer
> Let's call her, Dolé!
> Dolé won't answer
> Let's call her, Dolé, Dolé, Dolé, Dolé!"

And everyone joined in:

> "Dolé, Dolé, Dolé, Dolé
> Dolé, let's call her, Dolé, Dolé."

He licked her feet and her hands (hadn't she sworn to him that on that night, even in spite of the portrait? . . .).

Some of the people watching, thinking that they should offer some condolences, moved toward Capinche:

"Let's go have a drink in the corner store!"

And they all grabbed him and pulled him away. Perhaps it was the same bunch who had grabbed Dolé when she had been clinging to the dead man and shouting, "Oh, my husband, my dear departed husband!" But Capinche, swinging his fists, got loose and chased them off, tossing his head like a strong bull with menacing horns, and then he came back to kneel by the corpse. He defied them all, just like a dog standing over a bone:

"Dolé, Dolé, Dolé, Dolé,
Dolé won't answer."

He pulled off her shroud. He threw himself on the corpse, embracing it and kissing it on the mouth. He twisted around on Dolé's body like a serpent.

"Well, what did I tell you, José María?" cried the old Negress. "Have you ever seen anyone mourn a dead person like that?"

Capinche's movements became more and more lascivious:

"Ah, my *comadre*, my *comadre*,
how I love her,
Let's make love, my dear."

His movements became so lascivious that the horrified women hid their faces in their shawls. Those who didn't have a shawl raised their skirts to cover their eyes. The men grabbed Capinche violently, trying to force him to stop carrying out his sacrilegious desires.

They raised him up, but he was already a dead man, a limp

thing that they carried off and put down in the middle of the street.

Everyone rushed to spend the rest of the night at the police station. As for the corpses, the Poor House wagon had to come carry them away. And nobody went to sprinkle any water on their cursed bodies or to say a prayer for the peace of their souls, though their souls certainly needed some prayers.

And out of the limitless darkness, the everlasting night:

"Dolé, didn't I tell you that if ever I found you with another man that's what I would do? Maybe if it had been someone besides my *compadre* I would have pretended not to see anything."

"That's true, it's true you warned me! But I couldn't turn down a *compadre*, Evaristo, just put yourself in my shoes!"

Mambiala Hill

It was no secret in the village that Serapio Trebejo was always ready to try anything except working to earn his livelihood.

He always had some pretext or another, reasons he called "vocational." And since he was witty and loved to talk, and since he could play the guitar so well, it was really hard for anyone to refuse him whatever he asked. Especially since it seemed like he hardly ever asked for anything at all, just a few pennies for a cheap cigar and some rum, leftovers from a meal, and once in a great while some old worn clothing because he really couldn't go around naked.

He lived with his family in an old shack that nobody owned or collected rent for. An old shack that seemed ready to collapse all at once in a strong gust of wind or a downpour but kept standing in suspense. (It was just across from Mambiala Hill, where the road turns as it leaves the village and descends like a snake down to the coast among the palm trees.)

They lived off charity without many problems and had been able to eat pretty regularly – him, his wife, and his children. There were two girls with protruding stomachs and kinky unkempt hair filled with lice. They were filthy, lazy, always slouching over their cots, and old enough to be married off. The two boys were gawky and ragged good-for-nothings with no skills, no jobs, and no desire to find any. In short, they were all people that couldn't be depended on for anything.

Then one day, hard times fell upon the village, worse than anything they had expected, and food was scarce for everyone.

Nobody gave any thought to black Serapio.

Nobody could remember ever having seen him cut sugar cane on a plantation, pull a single weed, or even plant a sweet potato. In vain he strolled around, singing and playing his guitar, and then holding out his cockroach-eaten hat.

"Why won't you work, Serapio? Songs won't get you your bread anymore, lazybones."

The good housewives, lovers of justice, would say:

"The black fellow's at the door. Have the maid tell him that any leftovers today are for the chickens."

"Sorry, old boy. Come by some other day!"

And so his family began to suffer the pangs of hunger.

Mambiala Hill, which rose up not far away, pale green and shaggy, round as an orange, had a pumpkin patch near the top. But no pumpkins. Everyone knew that it never produced any fruit.

The poor fellow and his family had been going to bed hungry for several days. That morning, which was Palm Sunday, Serapio dreamed that he was in a pumpkin, exactly like a baby in its mother's womb but with all his teeth, and that he was gnawing away at the pumpkin. The pumpkin was jumping and running about, shouting, "Help! Police!" and saying that someone was tickling it and that it was going crazy.

"Could that be a sign from heaven?" he shouted as he awoke. And he made the sign of the cross. "What if I could meet the mother of all pumpkins today on Mambiala Hill?"

So, hopeful again, he tells his dream to his family, and then he climbs up to the top of the hill and looks around everywhere for a long time. Just leaves and branches and more leaves! In the whole thick velvety crowded pumpkin patch, there wasn't a single pumpkin. And he surely had examined every square inch of ground!

He looked and he looked. Then the bell struck noon, the time when other people sit down at the table for lunch.

Serapio wept, entreating God and Mambiala. Then he

started exploring once more, plant by plant, point by point, covering the whole pumpkin patch.

> "Give it to me, Mambiala, Mambiala!
> Oh, God, Mambiala!
> I'm a poor man, Mambiala!
> Oh, God, Mambiala!
> Me die of hunger, Mambiala, Mambiala!"

He was exhausted. But before abandoning all hope, he knelt down and raised his arms to the heavens. He remembered an engraving that told the story of a miracle, and he began to tell it to the heavens.

The heavens paid no attention. No pumpkins rained down on his head. Serapio was overwhelmed with despair and let himself fall face down on the earth. He wept all the tears in his eyes, and when he got up to leave, there beside him he saw a little red pottery cooking pot, on which the sun's rays glowed like molten gold. The most graceful and youthful pot that had ever come from a potter's hands! A very nice pot, so nice that it inspired joy and made you want to caress it. So he spoke to it as if that were the most natural thing in the world to do, and as if the pot could understand him and comfort him.

"How pretty you are! And how round! And brand new! Who brought you here? Some poor fellow like me, looking for pumpkins?"

And then he sighed,

"What's your name, my little chubby black honey?"

And then, twisting its hips coquettishly, it answered:

"Me name is Good Cook Pot!"

"Hunger must be making me hear things," thought Serapio. "What's your name? Are you the one speaking, or is it me and my double, one sane and the other crazy, but both starving?"

"Good Cook Pot."

"Well, then, cook up something for me."

And then the little pot leaped up and turned in the wind. It spread a lovely white tablecloth out on the grass, and using an elegant table service (silver knives and forks, if you please!), served a magnificent lunch to the poor fellow who didn't know how to use any utensils other than his own fingers. He ate until he could say only "oof!" and he drank until Mambiala Hill itself became unsteady. The hill lifted off from the earth. It was like a balloon that rose rapidly high into the blue sky, higher and higher, until old black Serapio, clinging tightly to some bushes so as not to fall off, went to sleep.

When the sun had lost its strength, Serapio went home, holding the cooking pot under his arm.

His poor starving family was waiting. As soon as they saw him they began to shout, "A pumpkin! A pumpkin!" But he made a strange gesture, a gesture that nobody had ever seen him use before, and so they had trouble understanding. But finally when he got close they realized that he meant "No!" Consternation spread over the faces of the poor misfortunate family, for they had gotten through another day on sugar water, hoping for a Mambiala miracle. They turned on Serapio, accusing him of eating the pumpkin for himself – up there he had taken advantage of the fact that nobody could see him! Only the mother, a tall dried-up old woman who had seen everything under the sun, didn't move or get excited upon hearing the man's footsteps. She stayed seated on her stool. Hunger had turned her to wood, or maybe she was made of wood, Mama Tecla.

She never spoke. Well, sometimes, confusedly, she grumbled to herself or gave brusque and unintelligible answers to someone who was visible only to her and who seemed to annoy her with useless questions. They must have been in total agreement, for whatever Ma Tecla mumbled as she looked at him, scarcely moving her lower lip, where an unlit cigarette butt hung, she seemed to be saying:

"You don't have to say any more – I know full well!"

Most of the time, mute and stiff in her miserable corner, she was nothing more than an object that expressed intensely in its abstraction absolutely nothing at all.

And nobody ever paid attention to her. It was even unusual for anyone to remember to slip her some of the leftover scraps, when there were any.

With her long bony fingers, Ma Tecla would squeeze the leftovers together, form them into a ball, then swallow them mechanically without even taking the trouble of tasting or even chewing them. Her indifference was a supreme form of contempt.

"Let's invite all the neighbors to come stuff themselves tonight," the fellow ordered, showing off the cooking pot proudly. But one of the girls, who had the mumps, said:

"Stuff themselves with what? With rats? That's the limit! Did you hear? Papa's gone crazy!"

And nobody would obey him. He himself had to go invite all his buddies and round up as best he could planks and sawhorses for tables. Some saw it as a joke, some were simply curious, and the guests didn't wait to be asked twice. But most of them were sensible people, and when they saw the table spread across the road and noticed the empty little cooking pot standing in the middle of the table with no food in sight, they felt like fools and started to walk off without listening to any explanations.

Serapio had real trouble bringing them back.

"Say, friends, it's a banquet for chameleons, who, as you know, can eat air!" joked Cesáreo Bonachea, the crippled fellow who had worked in the sugar mill boilers and was always quick to make jokes. "Open up your mouths and let the flies buzz in!"

But at that moment, Serapio bowed respectfully to the cooking pot and began to speak, saying in a sweet voice:

"What is your name?"[1]

"Good Cook Pot."

"Well then, since you can do it so well, my pretty one, make a meal for all these people!"

Those watching had hardly recovered from their astonishment when the pot had covered the table with the most amazing tasty and appetizing dishes. What chickens! What stuffed turkeys! What paté! And there were hams, meats, fruits, and pastries of all kinds! Everything was delicious, and there was plenty of it!

The whole village was fed, and everyone got drunk on the delicious wine that bubbled up incessantly from a kind of little spring in the bottom of each glass.

They danced all night, and dancing all the next day and into the next night was inevitable.

The feasting continued just as magnificently, at all hours of the day. And so Serapio the beggar became the beloved benefactor of the whole region. Everyone, even his closest relatives, called him Don Serapio without realizing it. And as he heard them call him "Don," as his stomach grew larger (worthy of a gold pocket watch and a diamond pin), he felt that something new in his soul was trying to communicate a message in a language as obscure for him as were Ma Tecla's grunts. And she continued to sit nailed to her stool in the same old silence, staring with those same hard, unfeeling eyes.

1. *Haciéndole "moforivale"* is a respectful greeting that blacks belonging to the Lucumí religion use when addressing their *orishas* (author's note).

The story spread far and wide, and people heard about it in all five regions of the world. It even appeared in the newspapers, and the pope, recognizing a miracle, hurriedly sent a pumpkin encyclical, asking them not to do any more miracles without his consent.

In the meantime, pilgrims had stripped bald Mambiala Hill. But when good luck smiles suddenly on a poor man, it's unusual for it not to bring along with it a curse of the same magnitude.

And indeed, rich people came to dine at Serapio's house. During dessert, one of them, whose beard was as shiny as his shoes, said, "I'll give you more than three hundred good fertile acres of sugar cane for your cooking pot."

"No, sir," answered Serapio. For he had all the sugar he needed, not to mention the scrapings and molasses.

"As for me," said another important man, belching elegantly, "I'll give you one of my coffee plantations."

"And I," said the director of the shipping company, a well-respected slave trader, "I'll give you my schooner *The Gull*, the most beautiful of all that skim the seas, with their loads of 'ebony.'"

And among these rich people there was a millionaire moneylender, a fellow named Don Cayetano, Marquis of Zarralarraga, who, so as not to lose any profits, would sell the hair, the teeth, the fat, and the bones of his dead slaves. And he sat there calculating, calculating in his stone-hard head, eating all the while.

"As for me," he finally said, thinking about the monopoly on the world food supply, "I'll give you a million pesos, and not a cent more, for your 'Good Cook.'"

When the fellow heard "a million pesos," he raced off to find the notary and dragged him back to his house.

On the spot, a sales contract was drawn up. At the bottom

of the sheet, with a sun like a fried egg stamped on it and a ribbon attached, Zarralarraga scrawled his illustrious name: with swirls and whirls, and three grandiloquent curves tied together with one bow.

"Please sign here, Don Serapio."

"But I don't know how to write," said Serapio, realizing it for the first time in his life. "And I just remembered too that I don't know how to read either."

"That doesn't matter. It's a deal among gentlemen."

Well. The document was worthless – because Zarralarraga that very night slipped on a mango peel as he got down from his carriage. And the cooking pot broke. And black Serapio, who already pictured himself in a top hat and dinner jacket, with a diamond ring on each finger and gold teeth, riding around in his carriage during the day and sleeping at night on a featherbed, poor black Serapio was as poor again as the day he was born.

As the days passed by bitterly, with the memory of his newly lost happiness still so fresh in his mind, one morning Serapio, whose stomach was touching his backbone, looked over toward Mambiala.

"Who knows," he said to his daughters, whom he could have dressed in silk and who now were barefoot and whose backsides were showing, "Who knows? Compassionate Mambiala might produce another little miracle for us. Even if I can't find another cooking pot, maybe I'll find a pumpkin."

So he climbed back up the hill. There weren't any pumpkin plants at all. Just a few blades of grass between the rocks.

> "Oh, God, Mambiala!
> Mambiala, leave it, Mambiala!
> Poor me, Mambiala!
> Oh, God, Mambiala . . .
> Me die of hunger, Mambiala, Mambiala!"

Groaning and moaning, he sang out his prayers, not even hoping for anything anymore, when the big toe on his right foot struck a cane covered with manatee leather.

"What's your name," he asked immediately, hugging it joyously to himself.

"Mistah Manatee! The good Sharer!" answered the whip, with the rasping voice of a rough man with a bad temper.

"Well, then, share with me, Mr. Manatee."

But Manatee pulled loose, and fulfilling his duties, he began to whip Serapio. "Whish, whish." And he would probably have whipped him to death if the poor fellow, after running halfway down the hillside under the relentless blows, hadn't managed between blows, as he was spitting out a couple molars here and a canine there, to say, "That's enough, enough, Mr. Manatee!"

Then the whip suddenly stopped and calmly stood beside him, awaiting his orders.

"What should I do?" wondered the poor man, counting the lumps he felt on his forehead. "I'm not sure it's prudent to introduce this Mr. Manatee to my family (although they all really need it). When I took Good Cook home, everyone stuffed themselves. Neither the pot nor I held them back! Shouldn't they also share in the whipping?"

Down on the road his impatient family was waiting. They had alerted their neighbors and friends. They were so sure that he wouldn't come back empty-handed!

"The cooking pot! The cooking pot!" they shouted as soon as they saw him coming, walking with a strange gait that they hadn't seen before.

"Do we have guests for dinner?"

"Yes, a few."

"Well then, go invite the mayor, the judge, the priest, the notary, and all the authorities! And also that fellow Mr. Zarralarraga, who bought the pot from me. Nobody must be absent; there's enough for everyone! Oh, my pretty one! And don't forget the doctor and the undertaker!"

The news quickly spread that Serapio had come back from Mambiala with something else miraculous. And that showed clearly that God gives double protection to those who are lazy and that we should never get discouraged but rather follow Serapio's example. Following his orders, they set up a long table in the middle of the road, and people came from far and wide to see the new miracle.

The rich and the important people showed up first. They all sat down, green with envy, with Zarralarraga in the place of honor.

The unruly crowd stood around the table, expecting to gorge themselves, to drink and to dance madly. Serapio noticed that people were calling him "Don Serapio" again.

"Hey, that's not a cooking pot! It looks like a cane!" grumbled an old woman. And wrapping her cloak around her, she went back to her house, remembering that she had left some beans on the fire and that they could burn.

"Get ready!" shouted Serapio finally, putting the cane down in the middle of the table. "Everyone hold still!"

"Papa, I want some ham!"

And his daughters said, "Papa, I want some chicken!"[2]

"Nobody move!"

There was a moment of silence, an open-eyed silence, a breath-holding silence.

Serapio moved away. As far as he could.

"Sir!"

He climbed up in a tree. But they all kept their eyes on the table. They were hypnotized.

2. In the French version, the girls say the Afro-Cuban words: "*Engombe. Titini engombe!*"

Hidden in the foliage, Serapio called out in a voice that he couldn't keep from quavering a little, "The one on the table, what is his name?"

"Mistah Manatee, the Sharer."

"Well then, Mr. Manatee, you must share equally!"

Pákata! Pákata! Pákata!

And the whipping began! What a licking! What a hiding! Swing that whip, Manatee! Nothing could be heard but that "pákata, pákata, pákata," sharp and quick as it fell on all those astonished people whose heads were suddenly filled with exploding stars.

In less than a second, the whipping whirlwind had swept the crowd away. Everyone scampered away as fast as they could, their tails blistered from the heat.

Blows landed most heavily on the ribs of the important people. No sooner did they land on the closest people than they attacked those farthest away who were trying to sneak off to shelter. Everyone fell down in heaps, all over each other. Their flesh was bleeding and their bones broken. And Serapio, hanging on to his branch and shaking it with pleasure, just like his ancestor Mr. Monkey, egged on his servant:

"Keep up the good work, Mr. Manatee! Be hard on the mayor, for all the fines he gives out! Harder and harder! And on his head! And don't forget the moneylender. And the policemen. Don't spare their faces!"

Once all the authority figures were spread out on the ground groaning their last, Manatee went into the shack where the man's children had sought refuge near the imperturbable Ma Tecla who was all curled up on her stool.

Every time he struck her, Ma Tecla would say to the other person, that invisible person, as she opened her white eyes a little wider:

"Yes, I know. Yes, I know."

That's when the little house knew that it was time to collapse.

When Serapio saw that everyone was lifeless – Zarralarraga with his huge diagonal mouth, his nose like an eggplant, one eye hanging like a tear, and his hard head turned into a mush of brain and bone chips; Serapio's four kids torn into pieces; the old woman dead, still stiffly seated on her stool in the ruins, and all the blood that the earth was swallowing up, glugglug, he picked up his stick and left the area.

"That was a little too much, Mr. Manatee!"

He wandered here and there all night, leaning on his cane, led by his cane.

"Alas, Mambiala, what a splendid gift! I wasn't asking for that much, Mambiala, Mambiala! A poor fellow like me who never had it in for anyone now must go on the road like this after a whipping. Oh, Mambiala, Mambiala! What is left for me to do now? Not even one of those parasites to feed!"

Day was breaking. Birds were beginning to sing in the quivering dawn of the trees. He found himself sitting at the edge of a well, and the well was exhaling its long-held coolness, its smell of hidden water, of damp stones protected from the sun. He looked in, and the water beckoned.

"Yes," said Serapio, "it's time to rest."

And he dropped the cane into the well. And then he jumped in himself.

It was the Yaguajay Well.

All the black women knew this story. They would tell it to their children, who, hypnotized with fear, would go throw stones into the deep silence. And they would spit on their faces in the water, and stare, stare untiringly at the Soul of the Well – that drowned person whom they could never see but who was down there in the bottom, clear at the bottom, and could see them quite well.

At night, the well – the Dead Man – would wake them up by making the frogs croak in the holes in his skull. The children would return to the well – in their dream bodies – drawn by the mystery, by the pleasures of fear, to look one more time, to break the deep dark mirror, the pupil round as a plate one more time with a stone. And to spit, leaning dangerously over the edge in the shadows, on that calm irresistible presence. Oh! Nothing could beat the Yaguajay Well at night! The drowned man would rise to the surface of the still water, climbing silently up the silence.

A muffled clapping of the water, churning up the fallen stars, and the dead man, turning over and over in desperation with his two hands outstretched, would rise up through the fragrance of mint. The black women had seen him, and he always moved away from the well at dusk.

Too late to get away, too late for anyone to hear their cries, alone in their dreams, they couldn't get away. Hands appearing over the edge of the well grabbed them, hands cold and hard like stones, and pulled them down into the frightful depths filled with untellable secrets.

The Easy Life

Once there was a man, lazy from birth, who married a lazy woman. She wouldn't sweep, wash, or even iron.

They had a child without really trying. They lived happily, doing nothing, nothing at all that required any effort. Sleeping like logs, singing and dancing, that's how they spent their time. Everybody else was heading slowly toward the end of their lives weighted down with work and fatigue, but these lazy people had everything they needed and always had enough to eat.

However, the man got old, without bitterness and without even realizing it. So did the woman. And the child became a man, a big solid fellow, as big as a pillar of the night.

And he never lifted a finger.

He always said that he was tired. And "Why do that?" And "What does that have to do with me?" And he would drag himself around everywhere – when he wasn't dancing – just like his father, and just like his mother.

The lazy old man had a cousin he didn't remember. A distant cousin, distant like everything that belonged to the lazy fellow. And that cousin who had no father, no mother, no brothers, no wife, no children, nothing but a nice fertile little plot of land, he just died. Just up and died, without even suffering.

His friends laid him out and attended the wake and wept for him in good old African tradition. (They tied a white handkerchief around his jaws as if he had a toothache.) They walked around his body several times, saying:

> "The cart maker turns, he turns,
>   Oh, and the cart turns too."

They recited "Our Father" and "Mary, Queen of Grace!" And they sang:

"Embámbálele, embámbálele, y tú-tú bamba, embámbálele!" And:

> "Oh! Imbariya, ta amimian túmba, Aínbariyaya!
> (My God, look with favor upon my brother lying here!)"

The old-timers told stories until the rooster crowed, and after pouring several gourds of water behind the corpse so that his spirit would stay refreshed as it ventured into the next life, they carried him off to the cemetery.

And the lazy man, who counted on nothing but expected everything, found himself the owner of a lush field.

Having something of their own, like everyone else, was so foreign to those lazy folk that for a few days they thought that they had a lot to do. So all three of them went to hoe the field – though they were looking more than working! – complaining all the time of the sore muscles that the excessive work caused them. But they soon grew weary. So weary that they abandoned the property completely.

One day someone came to tell them that the totíes[1] were eating their corn.

The old man shouted, "I'm going to shoot them right away!"

And the next morning he sent his son, who left with a borrowed gun and lay down on his back to watch.

He was just beginning to fall asleep when the *mayitos*[2] flocked in. They weren't totíes at all. Poor birds! They get the bad reputation, but it's the *mayitos* who stuff their stomachs.

---

1. Totíes are blackbirds (*Dives atroviolaceus*). There is a Cuban saying that may have racial overtones: "The totí is guilty of everything."

2. The *mayito* is also a blackbird (*Agelaius humeralis*), but is smaller than the totí.

A huge flock of *mayitos*, led by their chief, hopped around drunkenly three times, not expecting to find a man there, much less a giant with a gun. And the man yawned, stretched out about twice his own length, rubbed his eyes to get the sleep out, and aimed angrily at the little chief.

His movements were about to panic the robbers ("What's happening here? Aren't we going to be able to eat today?"), when their chief, quick as an arrow, flew up to perch on a bare branch right in front of the enemy and said to him (and his clear, pure voice enchanted the man, the earth, and the sky):

'Tío!
Tío
Tío
Tío, tío kandenboka
tío kandenboka
tío kandenbo furumina, gandenbesú!"

And then the *mayitos* divided up into two groups, and their chief was quiet a few seconds. And then, with much sweetness, so much sweetness and grace that he caused the man to drop his gun, he said:

"Chiérre néné, chiérre néné.
Ie chiérre néné."

And leading his crowd of soldiers, he continued:

"Give me peanuts, chácháchá
Give me peanuts, chácháchá
Give me peanuts, chácháchá
Cha, cha, chaá
Cha, cha, chaá
Good buddies, eat!"

99

And they all began to sing in chorus, turning the morning into a most joyous occasion. And the big black fellow, throwing down his gun, began to dance too, along with the spirits of the air, the sky, and the green leaves, dancing to the music of the birds:

> Ariyáyá, Kinyánya!
> Kinyányáyá, eat, good buddies.
> Ariyáyá, Kinyányá!

The next day, the old man said:

"Give me that gun! It's all rusty!"

And he went off himself, determined to protect his property.

The morning was cool, ideal for sleeping. And then the *mayitos* flocked in.

> "Tío!
> Tío
> Tío
> Tío, tío kandenboka tío kandenboka
> tío kandenbo furumina, gandenbesú!
> Ie Chiérre néné, chiérre néné.
> Chiérre néné.
> Give me peanuts, chá chá chá
> Give me peanuts, chá chá chá
> Give me peanuts, chá chá chá
> Cha, cha, chaá
> Cha, cha, chaá
> Good buddies, eat!
> Ariyáyá. Kinyánya, Good buddies, eat!
> Ariyáyá, Kinyánya!"

A soft breeze played over the old lazybone's forehead as he lay spread out on the grass, his arms crossed and heavy with comfort.

"How great it is to sleep like this!" the old man thought as he listened to the birds singing. God be praised! And he allowed his soul to wander with the clouds. . . .

When he woke up, what destruction those nasty birds had caused during his siesta! He picked up his gun. But the chief of the birds, always alert, always moving, stopped him:

"Come here, chéché[3]
Come here, chéché
Come here, chéché
Que abukía kengué
Give him some manguancha! Give him some more!
Que abukía kengué!
Manguancha, give him some more, que abukía. . . .
Kitíkin!"

"Kitíkin!" The old man's heart leapt up with youthfulness. He tossed his gun aside. He danced until Night came, asked the *mayitos* to be silent, and gathered them under its breast.

And the next day, it was the old woman's turn.

She saw the ravaged field. It was a joke to her. But when she loaded the gun, the chief called out to her:

"You're even more *chéché*
You're even more *chéché*
You're even more *chéché*
Que abukía kengué!"

"Mayito, I'm going to kill you," said the old woman. "But before I do, you'll let me dance a little, won't you?"

And with the *mayitos* singing and the old woman dancing and laughing, they finished their work.

Soon, there was not a single grain left.

---

3. In common Cuban usage, *chéché* means "cool."

Nothing!

Night fell. The old woman looked at the Heavens, the Vast Indifferent Heavens! . . .

Then she shrugged her shoulders and went home to bed.

Apopoito Miamá

She had bright eyes and straight hair, did the mulatto woman. She was sensuous and festive, even more seductive than Oyá (the Candlemas virgin), quite a husband snatcher and still single. She made men crazy for love, and they left their wives for her.

That was her joy, and that's what she was proud of.

The poor married women. They were always too ugly or too worn out to pretend they could do battle with her. They feared her more than the Devil himself or smallpox, and cursed her daily.

One day, a couple from another town arrived in the village where she lived, and they seemed happy. They moved in almost across from her two doors down on Green Cross Street, in number 7, where there was a streetlight. Then Juana Pedrosa, a Chinese-looking black woman – nice and plump, friendly, welcoming, and very diligent – didn't waste any time putting on her mantilla and paying the new neighbor a friendly visit.

"Juana Pedrosa, at your service and God's! I've come to say that my house is yours. It's modest but honest. The third on the right as you go down the street, the one where the parrot shrieks: 'Long live the president!'"

And without missing a beat, she felt it was her duty to enlighten her neighbor:

"Oh, my dear child! What a terrible idea to come live in this hellhole with a black man as handsome as the fellow you brought along! May God keep him by your side to bring you happiness! Don't you know that across the street there lives a woman who can twist men around her little finger in the worst way? That mulatto woman, I say, that green-eyed mulatto woman who's always on the lookout and who spends her life buying soaps and lace in the Chinese shop. She's going to be excited and will sharpen her teeth to gobble up your husband. Be careful, neighbor! She doesn't rest until she gets what she wants! . . . I don't want you to say later that I didn't warn you. Nor do I want to have that weigh on my conscience, stuck like a thorn, so I wash my hands of it all. That woman breaks up every couple that she finds in her path, and there's not a black man or a white man that she can't twist like a glove. Oh, dear soul, if it weren't the case that I happen to be without a husband just now, I wouldn't be here blabbing like this on your doorstep. I'd be far away from that woman, because with my work I could earn my living anywhere. You have to hold what belongs to you on a short leash if you want to keep it!

You can ask around. I, Juana Pedrosa the midwife, I'm a good neighbor who doesn't lie, and hates gossip. And when things aren't going well in someone's life, Juana Pedrosa's not the one who will dig around to find out their problems. Although there are indeed some badmouths – there are always some of those – who might insinuate that she brought them some gossip. Don't let that mulatto bitch sooth you with her stories, that slut! I've given you fair warning, neighbor. When she comes over asking (and she's got the gall to do almost anything), "Neighbor, might you have a little oil? For I've finished up all mine. . . . Neighbor, could you lend me an onion?" slam the door in her face, because that's not what she's really looking for, that hussy!"

Juana Pedrosa snapped her fancy visiting fan shut and stood up.

"With that, your servant is off. All I can offer you is my poverty (Orula[1] is poor and everyone loves him, and I'm very honored by the consideration in which I'm held), but at least, my dear, my heart is big, so big that I swear on my holy saints that it can hardly stay within my chest when it comes to giving you good advice!"

"Me and my man," said her neighbor calmly, for she had listened very carefully to Juana Pedrosa and found her very polite although quite verbose, "we are united by the sacrament of marriage, just like white people. Our mistress married us, along with the priest, up in the capital. And nobody takes the sacraments lightly! If you don't keep the sacraments, you die in anguish, and in your grave, even if there's a cross planted above, you eat dirt. Although if the mulatto woman takes José María from me, I won't tear her hair out, I won't create a scene. But I swear that I'll make her march until she meets Apopoito Miamá! . . ."

So then Juana Pedrosa, to fulfill her duty, went straight to tell the mulatto woman what the new woman had said.

The beautiful mulatto woman closed her eyes, swung her hips, and began to laugh.

"Well, then. Juana Pedrosa, go tell her that her husband is mine already, sacraments and all!"

It didn't take long for the man to notice her at her window (she looked like she was made of amber) and to run into her in the street with her red kerchief, making splendid music with her wooden sandals.

It didn't take long for her jasmine and cinnamon scent to envelop him and set him spinning, because the woman smelled better than a coffee plantation. Before they even spoke to each other there in the local shop, she began to drive him crazy and take control. There's no worse magic than the

1. Orula is St. Francis of Assisi (author's note).

magic of beautiful eyes. That's how she got her hooks in him, that mulatto woman, by looking deep into his eyes. And the handsome black man grew sad. He stopped going to work, couldn't sleep, and couldn't eat. He didn't even smoke his cigars anymore. He was irritable, thinking and thinking about his neighbor. There was nothing he wanted but that mulatto woman and her sensuality!

The woman finally won and set him up in her house, in plain sight of everyone, and kept him locked up inside with her a whole week.

Then Juana Pedrosa ran panting from door to door like a panicky cockroach, saying: "My mouth is an oracle, a true oracle! What did I tell her? Didn't I say the woman would take that cool black man from her?"

Now, the man was really a good fellow at heart. When the mulatto woman got over her thing for him and put him out, he returned home. But his wife had left town. People say that he found a job in a sugar factory and lost both his arms in the mill.

A year went by . . .

Now the mulatto woman isn't stepping so high. She no longer buys perfume at the Chinese shop and no longer sits in her window. The sun doesn't shine on her house anymore. No more silk stockings, no more fancy scarves or serenades.

If you had seen her, you wouldn't have recognized her. She had been so proud of her shiny smooth hair that glistened like jade and came all the way down to her hips. People compared it to the Virgin of Regla's hair that Juan Kilate had made with a white woman's hair for the local association[2] of black folks.

Her teeth had fallen out.

2. *Para el Cabildo* was an association whose members usually came from the same region in Africa.

Her eyes no longer showed their youth, and dance had left her feet. The loveliness of her body had died away. She was skinny and withered up like a vine.[3]

"She must have leprosy," people whispered.

"They say that nothing can save her, not even the San Pedro water that the African healer from Barrio Azul gave her. And not even that heal-all water of the saints," said the neighbor women who could now all pretend to be sympathetic.

And they would add, "God must be punishing her for sleeping around because she was so proud of her body. Now she's rotting away."

Just as she was withering away, so too did the plants in her patio, the ferns, the basil, the belladonna, the *maravilla* flowers that had climbed to her roof, and even the twisted fig tree that gave such sweet figs also died.

The canary gave up singing. "How sad!" said the drops that dripped from the filtering stone.

Everything that had joyously lived around her was now practically lifeless, drowning in misfortune.

And the mirror that had been given to her by that high-living Galician from Rivadeo, the owner of the Four Winds Shop, when he left her to go back to Spain to undertake a regime of good red wine for his chest's sake, even that mirror was like soapy muddy water, a fog in which an old woman's face faded in and out, grimacing horribly.

Whenever the sun was beating down on Green Cross Street, you could see the glass in the streetlight and the blinding whiteness of the buildings shining as if they would burst with light. But the walls of her house stayed in the shadows. The house was continuously plunged in dusk's dying glow, and it made your heart ache. As if it were sick in bed, light

3. *Como bejuco de Altibisí* translates as "like a vine."

never shone out of that house, nor did any sound, not one voice to blend with the neighborhood voices.

It was the house of the Evil Shadow – of the living dead. A house with its window shut.

Nobody knew exactly when the mulatto woman left the village, and nobody could remember her.

She wandered along the byways of the world. For years and for centuries, she walked in pain on lonely paths.

All the trees refused to shade her and avoided her. The very ground she walked on sprouted thorns that pierced the soles of her feet. Even the grass and other soft things became as hard as stone when she passed. Every cool place turned to dry dust. The sun beat down on her back, covering it with sores. And the cold, needle-like rain penetrated to the bone to make her suffer more. She was dying of hunger but couldn't eat, dying of thirst but couldn't drink the water she saw flowing!

Covered with scabs, her body crawling with worms, she walked and walked, day and night, in search of Apopoito Miamá.

> Apopoito Miamá
> Apopoito Miamá
> Apopoito Miamá
> Apopoito Miamá
> I need to pay for my sins
> With what could I pay
> Mambelle! Mambelle, oh!

The well's mouth responded:
"Keep on! Keep on walking!"
And the paths were never-ending.

> Apopoito Miamá
> Apopoito Miamá

Apopoito Miamá
Apopoito Miamá
I need to pay for my sins
With what could I pay
Mambelle! Mambelle, oh!

Everybody refused to bury her because they saw that she wasn't completely dead, the earth having refused to cover her.

It was the Monday when people light candles for the souls in purgatory and bring them food. When the clock struck twelve, all the night dogs began to howl at the leprous moon.

A few old men and the women healers saw a ghost and the tormented air moaning across the savanna.

But not one had the courage to listen to what the moon was trying so hard to say, as if in secret. . . .

"*Endumba picanana!*"[4] called out over the savanna the voice that lives at the bottom of wells and stretches out through the silence like a shadowy serpent.

Apopoito Miamá's chopped-off head rested on a black velvet cushion embroidered with thick silver threads. It was Mambelle's gigantic pale head. . . .

Apopoito Miamá
Apopoito Miamá
Apopoito Miamá
Apopoito Miamá
I need to pay for my sins
With what could I pay
Mambelle! Mambelle, oh!

4. *Endumba picanana* translates as "a bad woman" (*mujer de mal vivir* — author's note).

"Come closer!" said Apopoito Miamá to the mulatto woman. Trembling, her hands clasped, she dragged herself painfully nearer.

Then Mambelle raised his eyelids – thick, green, wax eyelids that weighed heavily on him. But all he could see was the sky. He couldn't look out of the corners of his eyes. His open eyes were like two blind puddles of moonlight.

"Climb up on my head," Mambelle ordered.

And the mulatto woman obeyed, climbing as best she could through the woven ropes that made up Apopoito Miamá's hair.

"I need to pay for my sins!"

"Come to the middle of my forehead. . . . Come closer to my ear so that I can hear you!"

The woman was unable to speak. All Mambelle could hear was her fear grating.

"Come closer to my nose so that I can smell you better!"

But the poor whore was ashamed. . . .

"Come closer, closer!"

Mambelle opened his mouth. Inside was like the night of the earth, a gaping damp ditch.

The woman screamed, "Die? Oh, no. Die? Never!"

A crayfish heard her. The crayfish had witnessed the whole scene, and Mambelle, who couldn't move his head, hadn't noticed it.

Grabbing the woman's skirt with his claws he made her trip and fall. So, instead of plunging down Mambelle's throat and into nothingness, the mulatto woman fell to the ground and was saved.

Mambelle spit with anger. When his spit fell on the crayfish's head, the head fell off. Since that time, the crayfish no longer has a head, and that's why it has to walk carefully backward and why on its carapace it carries the image of Mambelle's head, of Apopoito Miamá's head.

The crayfish is immortal and wise. It treated the woman's sores with salt and sunshine and thus gave her back her joy, her youth, and her gracefulness.

Eternal *Endumba Picanana* . . .

Tatabisaco

Early in the morning the women would go to work the fields. They would sow peanuts, sesame, rice, manioc, and okra. The men would go deep into the virgin forest to hunt.

This one woman used to work all alone in her field at the edge of a lagoon. She had a young child that she carried tied to her back like a bundle. When she got to her field, she would untie him, lay him down in the shade of some small shrub, and start hoeing.

Now as the shade moved around the shrub, the sun began to beat down on the little black boy's head, washing over him in burning waves. Mosquitoes and ants bit him, and flies would crawl into his mouth. And the wind, as it rose, would fill his eyes with dust. He would bawl all day long. But his mother never stopped working. She didn't even hear him crying. The Water Lord of the lagoon felt pity for the child.

One morning, from the water's edge, he called the woman. He was ancient, his chest was made of greenish-black mud, and his beard floated out over the water.

"*Moana*,"[1] he said, "give me your son. I'm Tatabisaco, the Father of the Lagoon. Give him to me. I'll take care of him while you work. When you're finished, just call me and I'll come back up with him."

The woman gave him the child.

"Tatabisaco, Tatabisaco, Tatabisaco, take son!"

She couldn't speak very well, so she couldn't really thank him the way she should have.

Since that day, whenever she got to her field in the early

1. *Moana* means "woman" (author's note).

morning, she would stand at the edge of the still-sleeping lagoon and call Tatabisaco.

And, from deep under the water, the old man would answer:

"Tatabisaco, Tatabisaco, Tatabisaco
Tatabisaco, Tatabisaco, Tatabisaco,
You told me, Moana,
The rope and the cord[2]
Tatabisaco!"

Invisible, he would take her child from her arms. The woman never saw anything. Nothing but the water's colorless transparency . . . and the first stitches of the little fish weaving their threads at the surface.

She would set to work and stay at it with no rest until sundown. Then, when she called, Tatabisaco would reappear with the child. The woman would tie him to her back and hurry back to her hut, never stopping to chat with the women who were coming back in groups from their own fields.

She would fix supper. Her husband would get home from the forest. Then they would eat and, dead from fatigue, collapse on their cots and fall soundly asleep. The woman continued to dig in her fields as she slept. And the man's spirit went back to the forest. On the hunting path, with his magic bow and his huge knife unsheathed, the man's spirit would spend the whole night pursuing the elongated spirits of the fleeing animals. A dizzying chase, stretching from the forest all the way to sky's esplanade.

When it was time to sow seeds in the furrows, the woman gave Tatabisaco the gift of a goat. But she wasn't a good

2. *Kuenda y brikuendé* is, in the French version, translated as "*la corde et le cordon.*"

speaker. And she wasn't able to say the right words as she gave it to him. She said, "Eat the goat with the child and all!"

And the old man withdrew, deeply offended in his heart.

And so, that evening, when she came to the lagoon, she called, "Tatabisaco! Tatabisaco! Tatabisaco!"

She called many, many times, but the old man didn't show up.

The evening was still wide and clear and the sky still pure blue. The lagoon no longer reflected the sky and had become totally opaque and storm-colored. The woman, not close to understanding the water's wrath, kept on calling impatiently, "Tatabisaco! Tatabisaco! Tatabisaco!"

The reeds on the shore twisted and stretched strangely, becoming dark poisonous snakes. The rocks moved forward on their own power like enormous crocodiles with their jaws open. The "Guïjes," gray and weeping, children of the inconsolable rains and of ancient sadness, half feathers and half stream of feverish water, pelted her with their pebbles sharpened by so many tears. The lagoon, blood red, began to boil. And the voice of Tatabisaco exploded like thunder:

> "Ungué, wó!
> Ungué, wó!"

And the stern night rose malevolently from the lagoon, a night of mire and gore.

On the way home, the black woman met the other women who were coming back from their fields. She heard one of them singing, "The husband of the Moon's youngest sister killed her son and gave it to her to eat."

As soon as she got back to her hut, she slit the throat of a sheep, put it in a big pot, and set it to cook. Almost immediately her husband appeared, asking for his supper. She began to wail and roll on the floor.

He first thought that she was having colic or that maybe some mad dog had bitten her on the stomach. So he went to the well to get some water to calm her down. But she went out, too, calling the neighbors and wailing until the whole village had gathered. Whenever they asked what the matter was, she would moan and shout even more, and no one could figure out why she was in such despair.

Finally, it became clear that the woman's husband had put her child in a cooking pot and cooked it, assuring her all the while that no harm would come to him. Then the man had put the lid on the pot, and his son had said, in a voice like thunder:

"Ungué, wó! Ungué, wó!"

And what was speaking inside the pot was a sheep's head. The man was going to eat a sheep's head, which was really the head of his own son. . . .

When the man heard that, he too began to scream and to roll around on the ground like a soul possessed.

And all the women wailed and tore their hair while the mother dug her nails into her face and breast. The old and the young mourned together, weeping hot tears. The terrified children huddled around them, adding to the tumult. Some of the moaning women demanded that the man be put to death, for he had killed his own flesh and blood. The men and the elders agreed. But the chief had great respect for the man. He was such a good hunter and never came back from the forest empty-handed. He knew how to attract animals. Nobody knew their language better than he. He knew the origins, the history, the tricks of all the animals, as well as the song that could captivate them. (It's said that the Demon Bird of the Virgin Forest taught those things to him for a little honey.) So, before staining his knife in the man's warm blood, the chief gave the order to call Babá the Seer. Now the Seer lived a little more than a league away. He had a talisman that could command the Great Wind, and a deer's antler that could command the Little Wind. Great Wind would bring back to him all the words that people spoke, exactly as they had been spoken. And Little Wind told him everything that he had seen. So that, well before the messenger showed up, he had already started out and he knew everything.

"This man is innocent" were his first words.

But there was no way to quiet the women, who had smeared themselves with ashes and were sitting in a circle, their hands on their heads or at their waists, swaying to the rhythm of the wailing.

Babá ordered silence, and people could hear in the darkness a sound like a mass of falling water in the distance.

Little Wind comes and goes, and speaking to the Seer, whispers in his ear that Tatabisaco is rising and is about to flood the earth and destroy the crops. In his wrath, he won't spare a single human being, and this time everyone will drown, because he'll rise as high as the highest branches of the tallest trees.

Then the Seer ordered Great Wind to hold back the waters and dissuade Tatabisaco from carrying out his plans. He chooses twelve male and twelve female goats and takes everyone – men, women, and children – down to the lagoon. And there they celebrate a purification ceremony[3] at midnight.

Babá stands naked and rubs a white dove over his entire body. Then he calls out three times:

> "Tatabisaco, Tatabisaco, Tatabisaco!
> Tatabisaco, Tatabisaco, Tatabisaco,
> You said me, Moana

3. The purification ceremony is called "un ebbó" in the original.

Tatabisaco, Moana and you said me
Tatabisaco, the rope and the cord,
Tatabisaco!"

A calabash begins to float, and it floats all the way to the middle of the lagoon, where it stops.

"Ungué, wó!" Tatabisaco answered.

The Seer pushed the twelve male goats into the water. They swam out to the middle of the lagoon, where they sank under the water.

"Ungué, wó!" Tatabisaco repeated.

Then the Seer sent off the twelve female goats, which disappeared at the same place as the males.

And, from deep down, they could hear Tatabisaco saying:

"Tatabisaco, you said me, Moana
Tatabisaco, the rope and the cord,
Kuma Imbinbo yo, yo!"

And before the eyes of the silent and startled assembly appeared the Old Man with his quicksilver beard, like shining fish (for at that very moment the moon was rising).

The little black boy was asleep on the shoulders of Father Water; the big serene night cradled the boy in its arms. Tatabisaco said he accepted the offerings, that he would not have caused them any harm.

He reached the child out to his mother, but she hardly dared to take him or raise her eyes from the ground.

The hunter took his sleeping son and carried him away. As for the woman, she slunk off to hide, like an animal in the shadows, an animal near death, to hide far away and forever, and nobody knows exactly where. . . .

Arere Marekén

The king's wife was a very beautiful, young-looking woman. The king wanted her always to stay close to him, but she used to go to the market every morning. While the king was getting dressed, he would tell his wife:

"Arere, you mustn't stop singing. Arere, you mustn't stop singing."

The king was very jealous because Arere looked young, and he was getting old.

Now the king had a stone that the ocean had given him. Every time Arere would sing, the stone would also sing with Arere's voice, and the king would hold the songs in the palm of his hands.

The queen would go singing to the market, and she wore a very white gown with a long train. She carried a basket in her hands. The queen sang like this:

> "Arere Marekén, Arere Marekén,
> Arere Marekén, kocho bí, kocho bá
> Arere Marekén, King can' t be without me!"

Running like a cloud, she would arrive at the market:

> "Arere Marekén, Arere Marekén,
> Arere Marekén, kocho bí, kocho bá
> Arere Marekén, King can't be without me!"

She would fill her basket with many colors, and she would return to the palace running and singing, while the king was already getting impatient.

When Arere appeared, the morning, the street, everything

would rejoice, but nobody, except Hicotea,[1] would dare to look her straight in the face. Hicotea was in love with the wife of the king, with Arere Marekén.

One day the queen was coming alone down the road. . . .

From where Hicotea was hidden in a bush, he could hear the sounds of gold bracelets and of the waves of skirts and petticoats, like double camellias: The queen was coming again, singing.

"Arere Marekén. King can't be without me!"

(Meanwhile the king was watching and waiting in his palace.)

Hicotea came out on the road to meet her.

"Queen, may God himself bless you."

Arere was afraid, but she stopped singing long enough to say:

"Thank you, Hicotea."

But later she said:

"What imprudence! What if the king finds out . . . !"

"The king already knows it, and he will kill me," said Hicotea, standing before her. . . . "Wait a moment, let my eyes enjoy you, Arere. That's all I want."

Hicotea was young, and Arere could not stop smiling.

"Arere Marekén, Arere Marekén,
Arere Marekén, kocho bí, kocho bá
Arere Marekén, King can't be without me."

"Good-bye, Hicotea . . ."

"Arere, a little bit more . . ."

In the hands of the king, Arere's song was dying. Later, Arere ran too much, and her heart was trembling; she was

1. Hicotea is the turtle.

trembling in her song and in the cupped fingers of the king, her master.

"Arere, why did you become silent, Arere Marekén?"

"Today the road was full of puddles. I held up my train for fear of soiling it, that's why, my King, I forgot to sing."

> "Arere Marekén, Arere Marekén,
> Arere Marekén, kocho bí, kocho bá
> Arere Marekén, King can't be without me!"

The king was attentive in his palace.

The queen was returning alone from the market among the white flappings of her percale doves. Hicotea stopped her again, and Arere stopped singing.

"Arere! Why did you become silent, Arere Marekén?"

"Today I lost one of my new slippers, my King. As I looked for it, I forgot to sing."

> "Arere Marekén, Arere Marekén,
> Arere Marekén, kocho bí, kocho bá
> Arere Marekén, King can't be without me!"

The king was attentive in his palace.

Hicotea was hiding in his ambush. Arere was coming, running, running like a cloud. (And the king's guards were following her from a distance.)

Hicotea kissed the queen's feet.

"Come, Arere. The dew is already dry. . . . Already the warm grass contains the perfume of the sun."

And the hand of the king froze in silence.

But the king's guards arrived and captured Hicotea, and took him to the king. When the king saw that he was young, he said:

"Let's club him to death."

"Arere Marekén; Arere Marekén."

Hicotea died that morning from the clubbing ordered by the king. As she ground her corn and her coffee, the queen cried.

Finally the night arrived with its flirting and festive moon. Hicotea, cut in pieces, came back to life.

And who could have imagined that Hicotea's body was no longer coarse, but was hard, smooth, and nice to touch.

So many scars for Arere's love, Arere Marekén's love!

The Green Mud of the Almendares

The mayor issued a proclamation saying that there was not a more beautiful mulatto woman in the whole world than Soyán Dekín.

Billillo, a carriage driver, loved Soyán Dekín, but he had never told her so because he was afraid she'd reject him. No doubt she was pretty, conceited, and cantankerous, but he knew that he was no small potato.

There was a party in the Cabildo[1] to honor Soyán Dekín. The mayor attended it. Soyán Dekín came to the party like a queen, putting on airs, and wowed everybody with her beauty. She spent the night dancing with the mayor and with nobody else.

Watching her dance, Billillo's heart filled with poison. He couldn't stand to see her acting with such affectation and so disdainfully, but his eyes ran after her radiance and after the swaying of her hips. He always saw her dancing or chatting with the white man. She was even lovey-dovey with him.

What a mulatto woman! She should have been born to put on perfume and sit on a throne. She was high class. With her flirtatious silk cloak and her cotton gown, Soyán Dekín was very desirable in her apotheosis; she was ready to be the mistress of a rich white man. Later, among the Negroes, she would boast of being a white lily.

Billillo sharpened his hatred.

To prevent a tragedy, he left the party, but demons carried him through the dark streets of the city. The trumpet, there at

The Almendares River crosses the city of Havana.

1. Members of a particular *cabildo* generally come from the same region in Africa.

the Cabildo, kept the night awake. And Billillo, may God have already forgiven him, went to see the witch doctor of the Ceiba, who lived inside death, and who spent his days concocting evil deeds.

Soyán Dekín used to sleep late into the morning like a great lady. Neither the early street noises nor the arguments in the common patio of her dwelling could disturb her sleep.

Not until well after eleven did she even think about getting up, and just because of who she was, so pretty and desirable, she would do nothing around the house. It was her mother, an exquisite ironer, who did the chores around the house and who earned a living. Because she was conceited and beautiful, Soyán was always seated in front of the mirror or at the front window.

Soyán Dekín came back in the wee hours of the morning from the party at the Cabildo, but she didn't go to bed. When the street overflowed with the cries of the fruit and vegetable vendors and the Chinese fish vendor came knocking at the window, Soyán Dekín said to her mother:

"Give me the dirty laundry; I'll go wash it at the river."

"You, so beautiful, and after the party, why are you going to wash in the river?"

But Soyán Dekín, as if someone invisible were whispering in her ear, repeated solemnly:

"Yes, dearest Mummy, give me the laundry. Today I have to wash in the river."

The old woman never contradicted her daughter in the slightest, so she made a bundle with all the clothes in the house and gave it to her daughter, who left carrying the bundle on her head.

People say that the sun has never since seen a creature with a more beautiful figure, or a more gracefully swaggering woman. That morning, when Soyán Dekín was going to the

Almendares River, she carried in her walk the halo of the morning and in her gown the sway of the breeze. There hasn't been in the whole world a prettier mulatto woman than Soyán Dekín: a Cuban woman, from Havana, delectable, who washed herself with sweet basil to ward off tribulation and pain.

There, where the river became a creek and the water became a child playing on the shore, Soyán Dekín untied the bundle and, kneeling on a rock, started washing the clothes.

Everything was emerald green, and Soyán Dekín began to feel isolated, like a prisoner in a magic circle, alone in the middle of an imperturbable glass world.

A new presence in the serenity made her raise her eyes, and she saw Billillo, standing a few steps from her, in the middle of the river, armed with a rifle and motionless like a statue. Soyán Dekín was afraid: afraid of the infant water that keeps no secrets, afraid of the silence, of the light, of the mystery that suddenly became so naked.

"What a surprise, Billillo, to find you here! Have you come to hunt, Billillo? Last night at the party Altagracia, Eliodora, and Maria Juana, the one from Limonar,[2] were looking for you. . . . And I thought, Billillo, that you would dance with me. . . . I'm not telling you this to trick you, because nobody can weave a dance on one single tile like you."

But Billillo was not listening; he was absent from life. He stared fixedly off into the distance, and his eyes were glassy and detached like the eyes of a cadaver. Billillo's arms started to move slowly and stiffly; like a zombi, Billillo began to load his rifle, and then he shot into the air in every direction.

"Billillo!"

Soyán Dekín tried to escape, but she could not lift her feet:

---

2. Limonar is a town in Matanzas Province, east of Havana.

The rock held her fast. The creek bed was very close to the surface, and the pebbles were shining like the blue beads of Yemayá's necklace. The bottom of the creek was shallow but started to sink. The clean, clear water, which before was playing like a child at the shore, grew big, deep, and secret.

The rock on which she had knelt moved by itself and carried Soyán Dekín away. She found herself in the middle of a wide and murky river, and she began to slowly sink.

There was Billillo, close enough to touch but still oblivious to her predicament. Billillo kept loading his rifle and shooting it in all directions, and the water didn't open under his feet to swallow him, as little by little it was doing to her.

"Billillo!" cried Soyán Dekín. "Save me! Look at me! Have mercy! I'm so pretty, why should I die!"

But Billillo did not hear anything.

"Billillo, you are such a bad fellow. You have a stone for a heart!"

But Soyán Dekín was sinking slowly and fatefully.

The water was already at her waist. She thought about her mother and cried for her:

> Soyán Dekín. Dekín. Soyán!
> Soyán Dekín. Dekín, I hurt!

The old woman, as she skillfully ironed white stomachers with a thousand plaits, trembled all over with anguish.

> Soyán Dekín. Dekín. Soyán!
> Soyán Dekín. Dekín. I hurt!

The mother rushed desperately out into the street, half-naked, not even throwing her shawl over her shoulders. In tears, she asked her neighbors for help. They called a constable. He asked, "Who saw Soyán Dekín go toward the river?

They searched the two banks of the Almendares River.

The old mother kept hearing the laments of her daughter, trapped in the liquid ambush.

"Dekín. I hurt!"

Now the constable and the neighbors could also hear Soyán Dekín's cries for help. Everybody could hear her, except Billillo.

Only Soyán Dekín's head was above the water.

"Oh, Billillo, this is *bilongo*![3] My dear black man, good-bye. . . . I loved you so, my sweet saint, I liked you, my man, and I didn't tell you because you were so arrogant. I didn't let you know because I feared your disdain!"

Billillo appeared to wake up suddenly from his dream, a dream that had lasted a long time, or maybe his whole life.

The river had completely covered Soyán Dekín. Her immense head of hair was floating in the somber green water.

Quickly, Billillo, with all his limbs freed, grabbed Soyán Dekín by her hair, and pulled with all his strength. But the stones wouldn't let go of their prey. Billillo was left standing with large locks of hair in each hand.

For three days the women and the constable looked for Soyán Dekín's body. The Almendares River, however, kept it forever. People say, and Chémbe the shrimp seller saw it himself, that there where the river is the cleanest and deepest, you can see on the bottom a splendidly beautiful mulatto woman who expands the heart of the waters when she moves.

Soyán Dekín is there in the water's green pupil. At night, the mulatto woman surges from the water and strolls along its surface, without ever getting close to the shore. And on the banks a Negro man weeps. . . .

Soyán Dekín's hair is the green mud of the Almendares River.

3. A *bilongo* is an evil curse (author's note).

Suandende

He was jealous. Asleep or awake, that octopus in his heart gnawed away at him. So he took his wife and left the village. She was young.

He went into the forest and built his house in the deepest part, and then he felt calm. There he was alone with his wife. Like a clinging vine.

With his brothers, the trees, he could live in peace.

Years came and went, bringing nothing, taking nothing.

The man spent his time making snares for birds. One summer day, when the sky was white hot, the woman went alone to the river. The sun was in her skin, and she quenched its burning by diving into the water. She was splashing in the water when a man spotted her. He had come from far away, following the riverbank.

He was a shy man whose name was Suandende and who made his living by selling jugs. (He hid his face in his hands, peeping at her through his fingers.)

She saw him too. Completely naked, she rose innocently out of the water until it covered her only to the waist. He was embarrassed. Not her.

The man called out:

> "Ayáyabómbo, ayáyabón!
> Me coming in. . . .
> Can come in?"

The woman answered:

> "Yes, suh, ayáyabómbo, ayáyabón!
> You c'n come in."

The man took a step forward.

"Ayáyabómbo, ayáyabón!
Can look?"

And the woman, her skin glistening with broken water jewels, answered:

"Yes, suh, ayáyabómbo, ayáyabón!
You c'n look."

"Ayáyabómbo, ayáyabón!
Can come in?"

"Ayáyabómbo, ayáyabón!
You c'n come in."

He moved toward her, with the same unconscious sweetness as the flowing water.

There they stood, face to face.

He said:

"Ayáyabómbo, ayáyabón!
Can touch?"

And she responded:

"Ayáyabómbo, ayáyabón!
You c'n touch."

The man began to caress her.

"Ah, ah, ayáyabómbo, ayáyabón!
Can kiss?"

The woman raised her mouth.

"Ah, ah, ayáyabómbo, ayáyabón!
Can take?"

The woman opened her arms.

"Yes, sirree! Ayáyabómbo, ayáyabón!
Yes, you c'n take!"

And he carried her off into the bamboo grove.
While the water, innocently . . .

When the breeze picked up, the woman returned home from the river completely worn out. Her legs were weak and her eyes were pale. . . .

At midnight, the jealous man woke up. The forest was bathed in moonlight. Miraculously, the cactus flowers were blooming. He begged his wife for a little love, but she pushed him away, swearing she was very sick.

The next morning, the jealous husband went along with her to the river because she had told him that bathing in the river was good for that kind of sickness, and in any case, he had already finished setting all his snares.

While the woman undressed and slipped into the water, her husband watched her from where he was stretched out on the bank. And on the far bank, even though there was no wind, he heard the bamboo rustle.

He kept saying to himself, "My wife is sick," and tried to think of something else. But his desire kept growing in the stifling heat. He joined his wife, who refused him.[1]

Holding her by the wrists, he kept saying, "I want to, I want to." Burning with desire, he tried to drag her off.

She called out, "Wait a moment," and whispered something in his ear.

And the man was dumbfounded.

"Right here in the river?"

---

1. The French version includes the following: "He hung his shirt and his pants on a branch and joined his wife."

"Yesterday," said his wife, crossing her arms chastely in front of her, "it fell off."

Then her husband, heavy with sadness, spoke to the water, his voice cracking:

"Ah, how in the world could my wife's sweet thing get lost? Ah, it's lost, sweet thing, my wife. . . ."

She tried to comfort him and to warn Suandende at the same time.

> "Dear husband, we will look for
> Suandende! Andende súa
> Has got lost."

And they began to look among the pebbles and the reeds. The man would bring up a piece of bark, a handful of mud, a leaf, and show them to her.

> "The sweet thing is lost.
> Dear wife, look to see if it's here."

> "Suandende, Andende súa. . . .
> That's not it."

And then she suggested that they each go in different directions to look, so her husband went downstream while she went up:

> "Suandende, Andende súa,
> My husband, go look over there."

And she crept closer to the bamboo thicket.

Her husband had disappeared, stirring up the water, desperately looking everywhere, and moaning:

> "Sweet thing, my wife
> Got lost
> Sweet thing is lost!"

Suandende left his hiding place. He put his arm around her waist. She went along with him, calling out all the while:

"My husband, look way over there."

"Oh, God, how could that get lost?"

Suandende the jug seller led the woman away, back to the village.

There everyone laughed at the man who had tried to be like a clinging vine.

How sad!

Sokuando!

Sparrow was a real braggart. He brought together all the people of his race. Then he called Ox, with whom he was always bickering and quarreling, and announced:

"I'm going to cut all your heads off. And then I'll show you that I can put them back on."

"No," said Ox. "You can't do that."

"Pshaw, nothing easier. Just watch!"

All the sparrows were in on his plan, and they lined up in an endless row. All the sparrows of Cuba were present. Not a single one was missing.

"Are you ready, ladies and gentlemen?"

Sparrow grasped his machete and stepped up to the first sparrow in the line. The first sparrow calmly bowed forward.

And the butchery began.

Ox, dumbly watching, saw that Sparrow was indeed cutting the heads off all his brothers one by one.

"Esékere Uán. Sokuando! Esékere Uán. Sokuando! Esékere Uán. . . . Do you see?"[1] he called out to Ox, showing him each head he cut off.

When he had finished his unusual harvest so quickly and neatly, Ox said to him:

"Not bad. I see that you have mercilessly killed all your brothers. But I doubt you can bring them back to life!"

"Oh, that's the real trick!" answered Sparrow with delight. And he quickly began to put all the heads back on their respective bodies. Then all those brought back to life burst into song! (All he had really cut off were tufts of feathers. As for

1. *Tú ale?* (author's note).

their heads, all the sparrows had hidden them under their wings.)

Ox was convinced and filled with admiration. And so he called together all the cattle in Cuba and invited Sparrow and all of his crowd as well. After all, an honorable quadruped like him couldn't let a no-account little bird get the better of him. All the cattle came. Not only the bulls, but also the cows and the calves. One after the other they show up at the slaughter-house. Then Ox grabs his cutlass. They are all frightened. Most of them hesitate and back off (with no false shame) before finally agreeing to undergo the test of the knife.

"Esékere Uán. Sokuando! Esékere Uán. Sokuando! Esékere Uán. . . ."

The heads roll, lifeless, and blood flows in hot torrents.

"D'you see that?" cried Ox, straining to lift the heads (it's amazing how heavy they really are!) to show them to Sparrow, who is about to throw up.

After several hours of hard work, Ox was panting and covered with blood from his hooves to horns but quite pleased with himself. Finally he felt he had finished the massacre.

Sparrow said:

"Great job! I see that you have indeed conscientiously killed all your brothers. But I doubt that you can bring them back to life, because they don't have wings."

"Ah, but that's the neat part," responded Ox gravely as he panted and wiped his brow.

He started to put the heads back on.

He placed them on the necks, but scarcely would he take his hands away than plop! – the head would roll to the ground. Not even one would stay where he put it. And try as he might to put them back together, not one of the bodies got its head back, not one head came back to life on the body that it had been separated from. We've got to admit it, no matter how hard it is.

While Ox with his great patience kept on trying to accomplish the same task, Sparrow declared him beaten and began to celebrate raucously his great triumph with all the other sparrows.

To make a long story short, Ox tried to stick the heads back on for the entire twenty-four hours it takes for headless bodies to stink. Finally, although it was a little late, he realized what he had done.

"I've killed my mother, my father, my brothers, my wives, my children, my grandchildren, and my great-grandchildren. Not to mention my uncles and my cousins. As well as all my buddies! How horrible! How horrible!"

And so he walked sadly and calmly into a pond, and in the style so typical of his noble race, he drowned.

Now, the whole bovine race would have perished on that fateful day if one old bull and one skinny cow hadn't abstained from joining in that strange business. But they certainly watched the scene from a good distance. In fact, at one point, the cow got a little excited and said to her companion:

"Fantastic! Let's us go too and get our heads chopped off. Come on, hurry up!"

"Wait," answered the bull, holding her back by her tail. "We're a little old, you and me. We can't work anymore. That kind of fun is for the young and the strong."

And it's from that poor couple that were born the heifer and the young bull, who, united in honest common-law marriage, repopulated the whole country. Thanks to them there are still oxen and cows in Cuba, the beautiful island.

Ñoguma

In Mr. Tiger's house, there's no cook. Nobody'd look for a job there. Who would be a cook in a tiger's house? Who would dare? They eat whatever the cook brings them in big pots. And then they eat up the cook! That's what they've always done. It's their custom.

In those days, there was a carpenter named Ñoguma. And people said that he was smarter than even the cockroaches. At both cooking and baking he was a marvel. So he went to the tiger's house to ask for a job.

"Ñoguma, in that big mansion[1] all the cooks have been eaten up. Don't go, Ñoguma. May God keep you from going!"

But he wouldn't listen to anyone, not even to his good friend,[2] Ma Theodora. He wasn't afraid, and he was getting bored doing carpentry work.

Now, Mrs. Tiger has a lot of kids. And she hates to cook because it's such dirty work.

"OK, Ñoguma, get lunch ready. And be quick."

"Is *entete* (game) alright?"

"Game? Sure. Excellent!"

"How about *engombe* (beef)?"

"Beef? For sure."

"How about *enuni* (bird)?"

"Bird? Yes, of course!"

"*Susúndamba* (owl)?"

" . . . ?"

1. In the text the author used the Afro-Cuban word *munansó* and translated it in a note as "*casa*" (house).

2. *Comadre* is the godmother of your child. She could also be the mother of your girlfriend.

"And how about *chulá* (toad)?"

"Oh, no, not any toad! Toad makes you swell up!"

So Ñoguma put on his lily-white apron and lit the fire. The fire, in the fireplace, said, "I'm ready!" And a little tiger cub came nosing around. Ñoguma killed and cooked him. The Tigers ate tiger meat and pronounced it excellent.

Later another curious tiger cub showed up hungry. Ñoguma killed it, seasoned it up nicely, and the Tigers ate tiger meat, saying, "How delicious!" Every day Ñoguma kills another cub, and the parents smack their lips. "This black fellow sure knows how to cook!"

Up until the day Ñoguma killed the last tiger cub.

The peacock, from his perch on a branch, had seen everything.

"Today's the day," said Ñoguma, and the fire shook with laughter. "Today's the day when Ñoguma must leave and go far away. . . . Mmmm. Tiger is vengeful, and Ñoguma has no intention of playing with his teeth."

(The pots and pans were all there in a row with their fat tummies and their black bottoms. All very serious. And all with their hats on.)

And Ñoguma, winking at the knife, walked out. And never came back.

Mr. Tiger is out looking for Ñoguma. Because he's hungry and it's lunchtime.

Mrs. Tiger's looking for Ñoguma too. And calling her cubs.

Not a single one is around.

At dinnertime, "Where the hell is Ñoguma?" "Sir?" "My God!" And the Tigers began to wonder, "Might the cubs have gotten lost playing in the woods?" Big Tiger is hungry.

He's really HUNGRY.

Ah, ah!

Later, it's bedtime. Not a single star is missing from the sky. Sleep came back, but not Ñoguma or the cubs.

The peacock watches from his branch with his hundred eyes. Totally engrossed in watching.

Three days went by.

"Tu húrria! Tu húrria! Tu húrria![3]

The fire is out and the cinders cold. Tiger looks around. And sees the heads.

Twelve cooking pots; there are twelve cooking pots, and in them he discovers the heads of his twelve children. And the heads open and close, their eyes glazed over in horror, and they stick out their tongues, already crawling with worms. . . .

All the heads are really rotten. And they ask for redress.

"Woe to you, Ñoguma!" said the tiger. "How can I get vengeance?"

"If you promise to give me what I ask for, I'll bring you Ñoguma in handcuffs," answered the peacock.

"I'll give you anything you ask for."

"All right. What I want is different feet. Pretty silver feet . . ." and he whispered in his ear, "because I'm ashamed of mine."

"I'll give you pretty new feet. Real high-class feet!"

"Very well. I'll not waste a second. I'm on my way."

"Ñoguma, Titigumá, titirigumá, Ñoguma!"

Ñoguma was in his carpenter's shop planing a honey-colored mahogany board.

The plane said:

"Sigueñé, sigueñé, sile!

---

3. The peacock's call, in black dialect, means "you ate."

> Siguené, siguené, sile
> Siguené, siguené, sile!"

"Ñogumá, Titigumá, Titirigumá, Ñogumá!"

Peacock's screams, long before he got there, spread half-way around the world looking for Ñoguma. Over the distant green hills. In the valley. In the forest. On the river. In every secret solitude.

The peacock had perched on the highest branch, way up high, and from there he denounced the killer to the four winds, rending the firmament with his screams.

"Tu húrria! Tu húrria! Tu húrria!"

The cry crossed a grove of palms deep in dream. And went straight to the shack were Ñoguma was planing his honey-colored plank.

> "Siguené, siguené, sile!
> Siguené, siguené, sile
> Siguené, siguené, sile!"

"Ñoguma, Titigumá, Titirigumá, Ñoguma!"

The black man heard that someone was calling him from far away and at the same time so close, and he grew frightened, not feeling alone. . . .

His flesh turned to icy threads from his heart to the tips of his fingers, and his heart spoke to him about justice.

"Ñoguma, Titigumá, Titirigumá, Ñoguma!"

The voice was getting nearer fast, like a galloping regiment:

"Ñoguma, Titigumá, Titirigumá, Ñoguma!"

And suddenly the voice was really near, right there!

"Ñogumá, Titigumá, Titirigumá!"

And there was a plumed tail brushing over the dried leaves:

"Ñoguma!"

Peacock was perched on the windowsill and saw a man bent over his plank. His hand felt fear; the plane was afraid and whispered into the board's ear:

"Si . . . le!"

Ñoguma, without turning around, drops his plank and slithers like a snake disappearing under a pile of shavings.

The peacock looks around with his hundred eyes. Totally engrossed in watching.

"Ñoguma!"

Silence.

"Ñoguma!"

Silence turned into absence. Everything was answering but totally mute. Ñoguma was there but like a dead man in his own house after the funeral.

"He mustn't be here anymore," thought the peacock, giving up. And he left, once again slowly covering half the earth.

. . .

The tiger was waiting impatiently for him.

"Well, have you brought me that Ñoguma fellow?"

"No, but I did a lot of walking. I did see a man from the back, a carpenter. So far away it must have been at the end of the earth. Perhaps it was that Ñoguma fellow, although I just saw his back. He disappeared I don't know how."

"You idiot," roared the tiger.

"What did you expect me to do? I wore myself out calling him, but he never answered. A man seen from the back could be anyone. It might have been Ñoguma, it might not have been. Seen from behind, a man is always a stranger."

"In that case," said Tiger, pointing disdainfully at his grotesque feet, sore from all the walking they had done, "just keep your ugly feet for the rest of your life."

"Oh, Tiger, you can't mean that!"

Swish!

The Peacock hops from his branch and spreads his fan: "Tchít, tchriii . . ."

His body is covered with diamonds, precious stones, and fine metals. And how smooth! Sapphire breast feathers, emerald tail! The fabulous golden-eyed tail. Tchít, tchriii! . . .

"I'm surely the most handsome, I'm incomparably handsome. Nobody can match me. Nobody!"

But sometimes, without wishing to, this great lord notices his feet and then he shrieks desperately, stretching up on his spurs.

"Tu húrria!
Tu húrria!
Tu húrria!"

Hicotea's Horse

Hicotea was busy reading *Havana Illustrated* beside a stream where Br'er White Horse came twice a day to drink.

"Good morning, good morning, Br'er Hicotea," said the horse.

Hicotea stared at him over the top of his glasses and, disdainfully dropping his words one by one, he said:

"Horse-is-my-horse."

Br'er Horse stopped in his tracks, hardly knowing what to say. In the heat of the moment, caught off guard like that, nothing came to mind. But later in the evening when he came back to the stream, he shouted to the tortoise, chopping his words off one by one too:

"Hicotea-doesn't-have-a-horse!"

Some time later Hicotea appeared at the court, and he said to the king: "The-horse-is-my-horse." (His words gave rise to lots of comments.)

The king sent for the horse and said to him:

"So, you're Hicotea's horse?"

The horse didn't know what to say. In the heat of the moment, caught off guard like that, nothing came to mind.

He began to think. Then he went to see Hicotea and said:

"Let's go see the king. You owe it to me to set things right."

"Oooh," groaned Hicotea. "Unfortunately, I'm on my deathbed today. So I can't walk, Br'er Horse."

"If you can't walk, I'll carry you."

"Oh, but with all the pain I'm suffering, Br'er Horse?"

"You can sit back on my croup."

"But I'll fall off, Br'er Horse. I'll fall off."

The tortoise made a gallant effort. He climbed up on the horse's croup. Then he fell to the ground, like a hard, round stone.

"Wait a minute, I'll put a blanket on my back. That'll make it easier for you."

(But at the horse's slightest movement, Hicotea, all bruised and battered, collapsed.)

"Wait, I'll put a saddle on for you."

"But how can I ever hold on, Br'er Horse?"

"I'll put a bridle and bit on too."

"And what if dogs attack us along the way?"

Br'er Horse gave him a whip.

"All you have to do is crack this whip. That'll scare them off."

"Let all be done for the glory of God, Br'er Horse. If you gallop too fast, I'm done for."

And they started on their way.

> "Gogorín-kinyón-kinyón, kinyón!
> Gorín-gogorín-gogorín.
> Kinyón-kinyón-kinyón!"

Seeing them gallop by, the trees laughed with all their leaves.

Finally, they weren't far from the king's house.

"Get down now, Hicotea. What if some member of the court saw me like this?"

"Oh no, Br'er Horse. Not on your life!"

And with that he flicked the horse with the whip.

"Get down, Br'er Hicotea!"

And they began to argue. But the king, who had already looked out his window and seen Hicotea riding his horse, came out to meet them and said:

"Oh, you are indeed Hicotea's horse. No question about it."

Then Br'er Horse began to prance and buck and raced off through the fields as if someone were pressing fiery spurs into his flanks.

Hicotea, hanging on to his mane for dear life, was able to stay in the saddle a long time. Just as they were crossing a creek, he said "thanks," and dropped off into the water.

Br'er White Horse lost his mind and fled from this world.

He ran and ran and ran and ran until he came to the edge of the earth. And he rolled off into the darkness. He fell off into the depths of unseeing night.

Even when he was dead the White Horse continued to gallop.

Into the starry solitude, into the lonely dreams of the stars . . .

One-Legged-Osain

Okó ebín kuamín . . .

She was really tired, the newly married Negress who had cravings like a white lady.

"My husband, I would like to eat hen and *fufú*[1] that you've made with your own hands."

"Fix it yourself, you lazy woman!"

"No, you! You!"

"Chon, chon, obiní! Go get me some yams while I fix the chicken broth."

Under the hut there was a mound of yams. And under the yams Hicotea had settled, hoping to spend the rest of his days there.

"What luck! Never will I need to drag myself around looking for food! . . . Thank you blessed holy God, for granting me such a fine place to live!"

That's what Hicotea said to the Creator, thinking that he was safe in his cozy home, when he saw the roof of his den lift off and the walls begin to whirl around him. The Negress had picked the largest yam, the nicest and the most worthy of her appetite. Hicotea recognized the shadow of a hand – that beast of prey – and began to cry out like an offended landowner, a cry that can't be mistaken for anything else.

"Alá lubiaba!
Teregóngu teremova! Tére! Teregóngu, teremova! Tére!
Bosi lubiaba masere kuché ko mo aberiyéye! Palaba!"

Which was to say, emphatically, "What gall! Who are you, stealing my yam that belongs to me!"

1. Fufú is mashed plantain bananas.

Frightened out of her wits, the woman dropped the yam as if the vegetable had bitten her fingers. She began to run, not turning around, not leaving her eyes time enough to examine anything.

"What's the matter, Obiní?" asked the man, seeing her in such a state, ashen, her heart on her lips.

"A talk . . . a talk . . . a talking yam!"

"A talking yam? We'll see if it talks to me!"

He left the chicken half plucked and went off to get his yam. Muttering threats, he came near. On tippy-toes, however.

"Alá lubiaba!" the furious Hicotea started shouting again.

And the man fled just like his wife without looking back.

He went to the king's palace and asked for an audience.

"Sire. There's a yam that speaks!"

"Never has a yam spoken," answered the king, "never."

"Sire. There's a yam that speaks!"

"Well, in that case I need to hear it with my own ears,"[2] said the king, with annoyance.

The man left, followed by the king. Behind the king came the army with its lances raised. When they came to the hut and the pile of yams, the king ordered his most valiant soldier to get a yam and see if it had a mouth. And immediately they could hear horrible shouting, shouting that left no room for doubt:

> "Alá lubiaba!
> Teregóngu teremova! Tére! Teregóngu, teremova! Tére!
> Bosi lubiaba masere kuché ko mo aberiyéye! Palaba!"

2. In the French version this translates as "with my own ears, and not yours, for yours are ass ears!"

The king's most valiant soldier was afraid. And the whole army felt their knees weaken in icy fear.

The yam was speaking! The yam would roar each time a frightened hand reached out to pick it up.

The army wanted to flee. So did the king, but he knew his job and was intelligent and stubborn. So he thought, "Under no condition can we allow yams the privilege of speaking. That would be a complete breakdown of order."

So he urgently sent for Osain, who had three legs.

And Three-Legged-Osain arrived. Osain, Saint of the Herbs, the saint who knows everything. When he had absorbed the gravity of the situation, he tied a white handkerchief on his head and asked for three coins as silvery as three full moons, three shiny new cooking pots, three roosters, and three coconuts.

"*Olorun maye!*" he said. "Light the candle, soldier. And grab the yam!"

"Alá lubiaba!

Teregóngu teremova! Tére! Teregóngu, teremova! Tére!
Bosi lubiaba masere kuché ko mo aberiyéye! Palaba!"

The yam protested with so much energy and authority that Three-Legged-Osain said to the king:

"I can't do anything about it. Call Two-Legged-Osain. He knows more than I do because he's older."

So Two-Legged-Osain showed up with the Seven Basils and the Thousand Flowers.

He asked for two coins as silvery as two full moons, two roosters, two coconuts, and two new cooking pots.

"*Ochiche!* Now, soldier, light the fire. Crackle, firewood! And soldier, seize that yam!"

But the furious yam shouted out more loudly still.

Two-Legged-Osain spoke to the king and said:

"I can't do anything about this! Call One-Legged-Osain. I

wasn't even born yet when One-Legged-Osain was already old and wise to the ways of the world."

"Cán! Cán! Cán!" . . .

That was the sound of One-Legged-Osain coming as he leaned on an old stick. Cán! Cán! Cán! Only one leg. Cán! Cán! Cán!

From deep within the mountain came a sound like an ancient tree with a cracked trunk sprouting new growth. His shoulders buzzed with humming insects, glowed with the dreams of lethargic lizards.

"All I need," said One-Legged-Osain, "is one silver coin, one pot, one coconut, and one rooster."

"*Ochiche*! Blow on the fire! Down with the flame! Get back, fear! Now, soldier, grab the yam."

The yams protested. But then the old man shouted more loudly:

"GRAB THE YAM!"

Quaking at the prospect of feeling the yam's anger twist between his fingers, the soldier – finally! – pulled the first yam from the pile. It didn't have a mouth, and it wasn't wearing a tie.

"Grab the yam! Go on! Everybody at it!"

"Alá lubiaba!

Teregóngu teremova! Tére! Teregóngu, teremova! Tére!

Bosi lubiaba masere kuché ko mo aberiyéye! Palaba!"

"Grab the yam!"

Hicotea choked with anger. He roared:

"Ala lubiaba! . . . Lubiaba . . . Teregóngu tére! . . .

Meanwhile, the soldiers, their courage bolstered by numbers, obeyed.

Finally Hicotea appeared in the open, defenseless, and grumbling:

147

"Osain, fódde nure! Please forgive me, Osain! Forgive me!"

"Ah, you old witch. As if I couldn't recognize your Arara accent!"[3]

With his stick, Osain pried open the shell. With ferocious irony, he went on working Hicotea over until he stopped moaning – like a black slave woman at the feet of the overseer.

"Osain, fódde nure! Fódde nure!"

And the whole crowd went off in great pomp: the man who owned the yam, followed by Osain – "Cán! Cán! Cán! Only one leg! Cán! Cán! Cán" – Osain all covered with dust but with new green branches growing from his shoulders; behind Osain came the king and behind the king his victorious army. Lances upright, drums beating!

The tired black woman, recently married, ate hen and ate fufú.

The black man seasoned his yam. Now the yam was silent.

And then they lay down together and went to sleep. And the sun also went to bed. And then night went to sleep in the night, to sleep until a whistle would wake it up.

One small, round, intense eye appeared above a pebble. And then another one, on a cactus nearby. A severed hand about the size of a *romerillo*[4] leaf was moving the stagnant silence among the grasses. Tiny sounds began to multiply, the sounds of body parts that had been mutilated, killed, and spread far and wide beginning to seek each other out, to piece themselves back together and come back to life!

Hicotea, seated on the roots of the tree belonging to the Bird who doesn't sleep – Yo bibiíbibí! Teketebuká! Va bibí,

---

3. The Araras who were brought to Cuba as slaves were reputed to speak with a nasal accent.

4. *Romerillo* is a weed that cows love to eat.

Bibí! – patched up his veins (and his blood sang), readjusted his bones, sewed up his flesh, and put his shell back in place.

Over by the mountain where a long shower of stars falls from the sky, One-Legged-Osain – Cán, cán, cán – was limping along in the calm of the secret evening.

"Yo bibí, bibí! Teketebuka! Va bibí. Bibí!"

"Oh, Brother Hicotea," said One-Legged-Osain. "It was just a joke."

And the Old Man and Hicotea, friends again, gave each other a deep and meaningful look.

They could read in each other's eyes the secret of the four elements.

Hicotea built a fire and took out his heart. He put it on the fire. Osain nearly died laughing at the sight of the heart dancing and twisting in the fire, whole like that, burning without burning up, until finally Hicotea put it back in his chest.

They smoked a cigar, drank some coffee. . . . And the coffee filled the blue night air with its perfume. . . .

The Amazing Guinea

Devils were holding Rain prisoner in a big earthen pot, and Madame Misery, sowing strife, swooped down on the land of the rice eaters.

Food became scarce.

One morning, Br'er Rooster was tormented by hunger. He hopped over the branch fence and walked and walked and walked and walked. Br'er Rooster walked for miles and miles.

Just as he was about to give up all hope, he found – oh, what a miracle! – a lovely property covered with grain.

He thought he must be dreaming, or perhaps dead and in heaven, but he plunged into the field and ate and ate, thinking all the while that he was only dreaming that he was eating his fill. . . .

Once his gizzard was nice and plump, he ran off to find Sister Hen:

"God is with us! God was turning a deaf ear but has finally heard my prayers!"

The husband and wife went back to the blessed field – this time very cautiously – and Sister Hen also got to stuff herself at her leisure, almost to the point of being sick.

From that day on, the lucky couple feasted royally while the other poor, famished birds were resigned to starving to death.

Lily-white Sister Dove – she even had white blood! – swooned at the very thought of a handful of millet. She could barely stand up, and as stuffed as they were, Br'er Rooster and Sister Hen took pity on her. Asking her not to tell anybody, they offered to take her to the generous field that God had revealed to them, that inexhaustible granary. However, Sister Dove could never be apart from her husband, Br'er Dove.

Nor could she keep a secret from him or taste one bit of grain without sharing beak to beak with him. That's how Br'er Dove got to go along too. And in the waterless pond, Duck and his wife found out as well. And Sister Goose and her husband also found out, as did Turkey. . . .

"How cruel to let us perish like that! . . ."

Finally they all went to visit the land of plenty, silently and carefully, so as not to compromise themselves or to besmirch their good names. And in each stomach happiness reigned.

Oh! . . . But Guinea found out too!

"But why?[1]

But why?"

"But why can't I eat too? I'm just as good as you are, you selfish birds!"

"Because you are too noisy, Sister. Because you're feather-brained and would get us all caught!" replied Turkey with authority. And just as the dove was very courteously about to add her two cents, her husband said:

"Hmmm, hmmm! Don't get involved, my Dove, my dearest. To change the subject, how about a kiss instead?"

"Listen, cousin, I know what you want," said the hen. "I'll bring you back some corn in a bag."

No way. There was nothing to do but take along the guinea. She was making an infernal racket but swore on the ashes of her father and saintly mother – may they rest in peace! – to be on her best behavior as a real lady and not to give them away.

She began to eat here: "Tchi, tchi! . . . Tchit! Tchit! Tchit! Tchit!" then there, then every which way.

"If she keeps that up, she's going to get caught!" observed the Rooster.

---

1. The author's footnote suggests that the sound rendered by the word *¿Poqué?* imitates the guinea fowl's call. ("*¿Poqué?*" is a phonetic rendering of "*¿Por qué?*" which means "Why?" in English.)

"Hmmm, hmmm," said the Dove, disgusted with all the chaos and huddling near his wife.

"Time to get out of here!" said the honest thieves wisely.

"Tchit! Tchit! Tchit! . . . Tchitchi!" the clueless guinea kept on shrieking carelessly.

Now it just so happened that the *guajiro*[2] was riding across his property. . . .

Morning was spreading out like a fan across the horizon. . . .

The man surprised the guinea as she pecked here and there, here and there. . . .

He jumped down from his horse and grabbed her.

"You little rascal!" he cried. "I'll teach you to keep your hand out of the cookie jar!"

And he came within a whisker of wringing her neck.

"But why? Why? Why?"

"Because you're a thief!"

And he shut her up in the pen.

"Whoever speaks with that insolent rascal," he announced to the henhouse, which was watching with great interest mixed with disdain, "will have *me* to reckon with!"

"Pascal! Pascal!"

"No, my name isn't Pascal!" And he slammed the door with such violence that his dog Cinnamon ran away petrified.

Guinea climbed up on a perch to think.

"Now what, Yewá, Virgin of those with no resources, how can I get out of this mess? What's bugging this *mundele*?"[3]

The farmer's young son came to play by the chicken pen. She called to him . . . in human language.

"Come here, my boy! Come over here!"

2. A *guajiro* is a Cuban peasant.

3. *Mundele* in Kikongo means "a white man."

?

"Tell me, son, how do you like gold coins? Doubloons? Piastres? Crowns?"

?!?!

"Oh, my boy, I'm going to make you rich. I can sing so well that everything from the crosses in the cemeteries to factory chimneys dance when they hear me sing! Take me to Havana. You can say: 'This is the amazing guinea. She sings when I get paid and won't make a peep when I don't!' Listen!"

And she began to sing:

> Br'er Rooster came along and did OK for himself.
>> Oh, oh, Ariyénye!
> Sister Hen came along and did OK for herself.
>> Oh, oh, Ariyénye!
> Br'er Dove came along and did OK for himself.
>> Oh, oh, Ariyénye!
> Sister Dove came along and did OK for herself.
>> Oh, oh, Ariyénye!
> Br'er Duck came along and did OK for himself.
>> Oh, oh, Ariyénye!
> Sister Duck came along and did OK for herself.
>> Oh, oh, Ariyénye!
> Br'er Gander came along and did OK for himself.
>> Oh, oh, Ariyénye!
> Sister Goose came along and did OK for herself.
>> Oh, oh, Ariyénye!
> Br'er Turkey came along and did OK for himself.
>> Oh, oh, Ariyénye!
>> *Isé kué! Ariyénye! Isé kué! Ariyénye . . .*
>> *Isé kue! Ariyénye! Isé kué! Ariyénye . . .*

The *guajiro* and all of his farm hands came running to the pen when they heard her singing.

"This is the amazing guinea. She sings when I get paid and won't make a peep when I don't."

"That guinea has a voice of gold! Sing, keep on singing, my little guinea! You sing, and we'll dance. You sing, and we'll never have to break our backs working again!"

The guinea wouldn't utter a sound until the men emptied their pockets.

To Havana, they went to Havana. On foot, along the road, singing and dancing.

"Isé kué! Ariyénye!"

When they reached the outer walls of the town, the watchman appeared.

He was Galician. And he danced along.

"Hey! Everyone follow me to the watch house!"

And the watchman said to his wife in his heavy Galician accent:

"I've brought you a bird that sings more stunningly than all the bagpipes in my Galicia put together!"

He dug up a jar and handed over the coins that he had been saving for twelve whole years.

The mayor, out for a stroll in his carriage on Alameda Boulevard, heard all the fuss. And he came dressed in his scarf and pounding his cane to the "Isé kué! Ariyénye! Isé kué! Ariyénye . . ."

"Gentlemen, what's going on here? Ariyénye! You're having fun without permission! What's this place coming to?"

The guinea stopped singing. And here was the mayor wanting to dance!

"Let's all go to the town hall!"

And he opened up a pouch of doubloons. So the mayor danced, and the mayor's wife danced (they were Asturians, stiff-waisted); so did the watchman and his wife. "Isé kué! Ariyénye! Isé kué! Ariyénye. . . Isé kué! Ariyénye! Isé kué! Ariyénye . . ."

It wasn't long before the governor arrived with his blue blood and his big cheeks, shaking his epaulettes. He had huge feet, an enormous mustache, and a chest like an altar, covered with crosses and gold medals. A truly distinguished Spanish grandee!

"Isé kué! Ariyénye! Isé kué! Ariyénye . . . Make way! Make way! Ariyénye! But good God, what's happening? Oh, I can't help myself! . . . I'm in a dancing fit, clear to the hairs on my warts! What's going on? What a day! Ariyénye!"

"Something splendid, Mr. Governor, sir!"

And they all went to the governor's palace.

"Come out, dear daughters of my loins, and you, too, my wife," cried His Excellency. "Come listen to the amazing guinea!"

And he scattered about generous handfuls of coins.

The governor's wife, a nice plump and stupid Cuban lady, came dancing out through some red curtains into the room.

And everyone danced – the watchman and the mayor, the watchman's wife and the mayoress, the governor and the governor's missus, even his nine unmarried daughters.

Then, the king of Spain arrived on a frigate with his entire court, along with a white marble statue of Christopher Columbus, an executioner, and a *padre*.[4]

"Tell me, my many-colored subjects, what is that, the Mambi[5] rumba?

"Isé kué! Ariyénye! Isé kué! Ariyénye . . . What a sight! But, say, what fun! Ariyénye!"

"Sire, the guinea, the amazing guinea . . ."

"I'll make her vice-queen of my green Antilles, of my sweet Antilles! Gentlemen, let the merrymaking go on!"

4. In the French version it says: "with Christopher Columbus, Indébil and Mandonio!"

5. The Mambís were the Cuban rebel soldiers who fought against the Spaniards in the Cuban wars of independence (1868–98).

The king climbed the staircase without missing a beat: "Ariyénye! Ariyénye!"

The Queen, wearing her diamond crown and her ermine coat, wiggled her ass:

"Isé kué! Ariyénye! Isé kué! Ariyénye . . ."

And now everyone was dancing: the watchman and his wife, the mayor and the mayoress, the governor and missus, the governor's lethargic daughters, the royal-blooded princes and princesses, the counts, the dukes, the marquises, and the bishop of Havana, the army, the navy, the legislature and the Economics Society of Friends of the Country.[6] And even the parrot, the dog, and the cat.

The coachmen in the stables; the cooks, pots, and pans in the kitchen; the washerwoman and the ironing woman on the terrace. And the blouses, the skirts, and men's modest long johns hanging on the line. And the clouds. Everything was dancing.

At the palace gates, the doors, the lamps, and the night watchmen, in spite of the hour. And even in the park, beneath the laurel bushes, under balconies garnished with women, the grouchy, bullheaded captain who was responsible for the port and for chasing away pirates, he too was dancing happily with the bony, nasty, gristly, pitch-black woman called The Red Ant.

"Now," said the amazing guinea, "give me some space so that I can sing for all the people."

"So be it," said the king, "it's good for the people to enjoy themselves, too, from time to time."

"Long live General Tacón.[7] Long live the rumba! Long live the public administration! Long live the Constitution! Long live the fun!"

6. In the French version, "the Autonomous Assembly" is added.

7. General Miguel Tacón (1775–1854). He was a Spanish colonial governor of Cuba (1834–38), very unpopular because of his authoritarian rule.

The whole joyful gang let loose – mulattos, maroons, zambos, creoles, quadroons, blacks, whites, and yellows – Chinese – they all sang together, accompanied by drums, bells, maracas, rattles, and cowbells, and followed the guinea all the way, well beyond the Charles III Promenade, all the way to El Principe Hill.

The drums said:

"I's hot! I's hot!"

The whole town was dancing. Even the hated civil guard seemed human.

All the black fraternal associations came out, dressed in their three-cornered hats, their sashes and banners, carnival figures with their lamps, people disguised as devils, *congos, lucumís, mandingas, ararás.*[8] There were the little rascals from the Jesus-Mary brotherhood, adorned with their huge baggy pants, their pleated shirts with ironed sleeves, their Calañas hats and their colorful bandanas.

Isé kué! Ariyénye! Isé kué! Ariyénye . . .

Isé kué! Ariyénye! Isé kué! Ariyénye . . .

Up, up, way up on the Atarés castle, there's the guinea.

She raised one wing, Ariyénye! By the time anyone realized that she was gone, she was already back home with her buddies and was telling them her story.

Br'er Dove was scandalized:

"Hmmm, hmmm! That nervy flattering guinea! What a bad example for a sweet little modest dove."

Gander stood with his legs spread and had trouble understanding it all. All the fuss was giving him a headache. But Br'er Rooster, whose crest, spurs, and masculinity gave him the prestige of a boss, thought it his duty to scold the guinea:

"You're crazy, utterly insane! You deserve to have your eyes

8. These are Cubans from different regions in Africa.

pecked out, and you have the gall to laugh and even to brag! You wicked little guinea! When are you ever going to have any sense?"

"*Nunca! Nunca! Nunca! Nunca!*"[9] Br'er Turkey was nearly bursting with anger, and started gobbling like a truly punctilious idiot.

9. *Nunca*, an onomatopoetic word for the call of the turkey, means "never" in Spanish.

The Letter of Emancipation

Back in the days when animals could speak, when they were all good friends and when men and animals got along fine, the dog was a slave. Even then he loved men more than anything else.

In those days, when hours were long and when nobody was ever in a hurry, the cat, the dog, and the mouse were inseparable. The best pals in Cuba. They would get together near the port in the courtyard of a grand house whose stained-glass windows caught the dying reflections of the sea. There, at the foot of a laurel tree that had been beaten down with all its birds by the new times, they would often spend half the night talking.[1]

Once after Br'er Cat and Br'er Mouse (who was well acquainted with books and was quite erudite) had sung liberty's praises and spoken extensively on the rights of all the earth's children, including the children of the sky and the air, Dog realized that he was a slave, and that made him sad.

The next day, he went up to see Olufi[2] to ask for a letter granting him his freedom.

"Badá didé odiddena!"[3]

The Oldest Man of the Heavens scratched his head and thought for a while, wondering if he should grant the request or not.[4]

Finally, after shrugging his shoulders and spitting a black

---

1. The French edition adds "and chewing tobacco."

2. Olufi is the Eternal Being or the Holy Spirit.

3. "Wake up, old man, wake up!"

4. The following is found in the French text but not in the Spanish: "Because he had always said that right or wrong, each person should have what he deserved. And in that case, the Dog deserved his letter."

159

stream of tobacco juice, as he usually does when making a decision, he scratched his name on a sheet of parchment and gave Dog a proper letter of emancipation. That same evening, Dog was showing it proudly to his friends.

"Take good care of it, my friend," advised Cat as he was leaving.

Now, since Dog didn't have any pockets, he thought the safest place would be to shove it up his ass. But, after an hour or so, the rolled up parchment began to itch something awful. More and more uncomfortable, Br'er Dog had to walk stiffly, his hind legs spread apart awkwardly. He didn't dare make the slightest movement or express any feelings with his tail. The horrible itching flared up at the most awkward moments, and he couldn't stop himself from running off in desperation to rub his bottom on the ground, not thinking of the consequences. All these humiliating actions happened right in public, and everyone made fun of him. What torture! And on top of everything, he worried constantly about losing the document, or by not being careful enough, about making the document illegible and therefore null and void. Br'er Dog abstained from eating, but finally, unable to choose between freedom and his incessant suffering, he pulled the document from its hiding place and gave it to his friend Br'er Cat for safekeeping.

The cat realized how serious a responsibility it was to leave a manumission letter on a roof where it could be damaged by wind and rain, and he took it to Br'er Mouse, who had a solid house with a good roof on it. But Mouse had gone to the market to get some cheese and it was Mrs. Mouse who greeted him. So he entrusted the letter to her with all sorts of instructions. But, wouldn't you know it! Mrs. Mouse was going into labor. She took the letter in her teeth and ripped it into tiny pieces to line her nest.

Meanwhile, Dog had a quarrel with his master.

He said, "Give me another bone!"

And the master replied, "I don't feel like it."

Dog stared at the man, who was stepping forward with his whip raised.

"I need a lot more to eat, because I'm free!"

But the man said:

"You'll eat what I want you to eat. You were born a slave, and you're my slave!"

"No sir," shouted Dog. (And his tail wagged approvingly.) "I'm not your slave. I have a letter of manumission."[5]

"Well, bring it to me, and be quick about it!"

Dog ran to the courtyard, under the laurel tree, and called his friend Cat.

"Br'er Cat, quick. Quick, give me my letter of freedom."

Cat called Mouse.

"Br'er Mouse, quick. Quick bring me Dog's letter that your wife is keeping safe."

Br'er Mouse ran home.

His wife was sleeping, with seven newborn little mice, amidst the torn scraps of paper.

He hurried back all embarrassed and whispered into Br'er Cat's ear. And then Br'er Cat lifted his two front paws and for the first time – "Fffff!" – he extended his claws and pounced on Mouse. And for the first time Dog leaped on Cat and planted his canines in Cat's neck.

Lying on his back, Br'er Cat struggled valiantly. A veritable whirlwind of meows, slashing claws and teeth, eyes spitting fire, and dripping blood.

Tiny Br'er Mouse scurried off at some point to his hole.

Cat was in a sorry state and, with his fur all ruffled, he climbed up the laurel tree and then out onto the roof. From

5. The French version adds: "given to me by Olufina."

there, he arched his back and went on meowing and spitting forth his bile and insults at the dog.

Then Br'er Dog quietly returned, licked his master's hands, and lay down at his feet without saying another word.

The Mutes

On the first night, the moon looked like a thin strand of hair. On the next, like the edge of a transparent sickle. Next it looked like a slice of juicy honeydew melon, and then like a round millstone. Finally it dropped off into the night's deep mouth, where the Eternally Hidden, the person whom no one has ever seen and who lives at the bottom of the bottomless, smashes up all the old moons with a stone to make stars while another moon is on its way.

In those days the night was as dark as pitch, and Tiger took advantage of the situation to steal fire from a cave in Insambiapunga by dancing before the person guarding it.

The hunter wanted some light in his hut. At midnight he shook his eldest son's arm to wake him:

"Go to Tiger's house," he said, "and ask him for some light."

"I'm scared!" said the boy.

"You must obey me!" ordered the hunter.

And he threw him out into the darkness, into the dense night of those days when there weren't yet any stars between two moons.

"Knock, knock!"

Tiger was a light sleeper ever since he had stolen the fire. He would put it between his front paws and fall asleep guarding it, without ever straying off too far on the steep slopes of the dream world. And so he could keep feeling its living warmth against his chest and watching the flame's subtle movements that were subtler still when his eyes were closed.

(This first fire was only a very small fire. . . .)

Scarcely had the boy tapped at the door with his finger than Tiger, pretending to be quite old, began to sing as if he were complaining of a deep sorrow, of a wound to the body. He began to sing this song that mustn't be sung deep in the forest after the sun has set. Nothing was left of the song but the words. The dark wind of that moonless night carried the melody off beyond all forgotten things. Because of this, imprudent men were unable to bring back the exact memory of the song and repeat its words. . . .

> Tanifayoku. Teremina!
> Tanifayoku. Teremina!
> Oruniwayo teremina!
> Wayayé Oñiná teremina!
> Wayayé teremina!

"Come in," said Tiger, opening the door and showing him the fire.

"I'm scared!"

Tiger pounced and swallowed the hunter's son.

The hunter, who was swatting mosquitoes while waiting for the light, said to his second son:

"Go to Tiger's house and ask him for a spark from his fire."

"I'm scared," answered the boy. "Wait until dawn."

"Obey me," said the hunter.

Tiger was stretched out in his open doorway.

> Tanifayokum.
> Teremina!

"Grandfather, give me a spark from your fire. My father has sent me to ask you."

"Yes, indeed," said Tiger. "I believe you. Take this stick

with fire rising on it. Hold on tight, so it doesn't get away from you."

And he swallowed up the hunter's second son.

The hunter sent his seven children, one after the other, to Tiger's house. Not one returned home.

"I'll go myself," he decided.

Tiger had closed his door. His head was beginning to nod. Though he didn't want to, he was sliding down the path of dreams, leaving his body and the fire behind.

"Knock! Knock!"

"Oh, it's you, Hunter.[1] But the door isn't locked. All you have to do is push it."

"No," answered the man. "I won't come in. I'm scared. I'm scared. Good-bye!"

But Tiger didn't give him time to run away. Pouncing out of the reddish darkness, he grabbed him and gobbled him up.

In Tiger's stomach, the hunter found his seven sons still alive. Realizing that he had his knife in his hand, he cut open the animal's side, and one by one, they all stepped out through the opening.

The trembling man seized the fire, and they left silently under a black, black sky, a moonless sky that as yet had no stars.

And never again did they regain the use of words.

That's why there are people in the world today who can't speak.

---

1. There follow in the French version two sentences not appearing in the Spanish: "My stomach is heavy and I can't get up to open the door for you. I feel bloated and am no longer nimble."

The Watchful Toad

There was a pair of twins who wandered alone all through the world. They were no bigger than a grain of millet.

They wandered through a deep, dark forest in which the evil witch lived, and she paralyzed the air. And there was also the toad, who protected the woods and their secret.

Walking, walking, children of no one, the twins kept walking through life's immensity.

One day, a little perfidious path opened up before them and used its tricks to lead them to the woods. When they tried to leave, the path had fled, and there they were, lost in endless darkness that not a ray of light penetrated.

They slowly felt their way forward, not knowing where they were going, touching the darkness with their sightless hands. And the woods became thicker and more sinister and fearfully silent. It moved deeper into the entrails of the starless night.

The twins began to cry and that woke up the toad, dozing in his lifeless mud puddle, lifeless for centuries with no conception of light.

(Now the old toad had never heard a child cry.) He walked for a long time in the echoless forest – there were neither bird songs nor sweet rustling branches – and he found the twins who were quivering like the cry of a cricket in the grass. (Never had the cold toad seen a child.) The twins embraced him, not knowing who he was, and there he sat motionless, one child cradled asleep in each arm. His warm heart melted, and the children's dreams flowed through his veins.

"Tángala, tángala, mitángala, tú juran gánga.
Kukuñongo, Evil devil, new broom for sweeping
earth and heaven!

Cocuyero, give me eyes so that I may see!
Horror of dreams, let all tremble! I knock over la Seiba[1]
angulo, the seven Rays, Mamma Louisa . . .
Sarabanda! Jump, wooden horse! Lightning! Tornado!
Evil wind, carry it off, carry it off!"

The woods were pressing against his back on tiptoes and watching him anxiously. From the dead branches, ears were hanging, listening to his heartbeat. Millions of invisible eyes, with sharp, furtive glances, pierced the compact darkness. And behind everything lay silence's inexorable claw.

The guardian toad left the twins lying on the ground.

"No matter who suffers, Sampunga wants some blood!
No matter who suffers, Sampunga wants some blood!"

At the far end of the night, the witch extended her hands like rotten roots.

The toad sighed deeply, and he swallowed the twins. He fled through the woods like a thief, and when the twins were jolted awake, they said:

"Chamatú, chekundale,
Chamatú, chekundale, chapundale,
Kuma, kuma tú!
Tún! tún! Túmbiyaya!
Where are they taking me? Túmbiyaya!
Where are they taking me! Túmbiyaya!"

In the muddy stomach.
Dust of the crossroads.
Earth from the cemetery, dug at midnight.
Black earth from an anthill, because ants have worked dog-

1. The *seiba* (or *ceiba*) is a large tropical tree with magical powers.

gedly, thinking neither of pain nor pleasure, since the beginning of time. The *Bibijaguas*,[2] industrious and wise.

Stomach of Mama Téngue. She learned her mysterious work in the roots of the Grandmother Seiba, in the earth's womb for seven days. For seven days she learned the work of silence among the fish in the river's depths. Mama Téngue drank the Moon.

With the hairy spider and the scorpion, with rotten rooster head and with owl-eye, eye of immovable night, blood yoke, the Word of the Shadows shone. "Evil spirit! Evil spirit! Mouth of darkness, worm's mouth, consuming life! Allá Kiriki, allai bosaikombo, allá kiriki!"

Flat on her stomach, the old woman spat alcohol along with dust and Chinese pepper into the enchanted saucepan.

On the ground, she drew arrows with ashes and sleeping serpents with smoke. She made the seashells speak.

"Sampúnga, Sampúnga wants some blood!"

"There's no time left," said the witch.

The toad didn't answer.

"Give me what's mine!" repeated the old hag.

The toad cracked his lips and a viscous green thread came out.

The witch burst into cackles like a whirlwind of dry leaves, and she filled a sack with stones. The stones turned to rocks, and the sack got as big as a mountain.

"Carry that load away for me, over there, nowhere!"

With his weak arms, the toad lifted up the mountain and put it effortlessly on his back.

The toad hopped forward as best he could in the limitless darkness. The witch followed him through a broken mirror.

> "Chamatú, chekundale,
> Chamatú, chekundale, chapundale,

2. *Bibijaguas* are large ants, common in Cuba.

Kúma, kuma tú!
Tún! Tún! Tumbiyaya! Where are they taking me?
Tumbiyaya!
Where are they taking me! Tumbiyaya!"

And now the warmhearted toad was singing joyously at every hop:

"Saint John of Paúl
With one swig,
Saint John of Paúl,
That's how I swallow."

There, neither very close nor very far away, the toad let the twins out of his stomach. And the twins, again finding themselves in that unknown night, now that they were awake, burst into bitter tears. . . .

Then Toad's fat, ugly face expressed unbelievable tenderness. And he pronounced that incorruptible word, a forgotten lost word that was older than the world's sadness. And the word became the light of dawn. Through their tears, the twins saw the forest retreat, disintegrate in slow, vague dance steps, and finally disappear into the pale horizon. And soon the new day arose, the clean smell of the morning.

They found themselves at the gates of a village, in full sunlight, and went off down the white road singing and laughing.

"Traitor!" cried the witch, twisted with hate. And the toad, filled with sweetness, lay dreaming in his mud puddle, dreaming in the purest waters. . . .

The witch came to kill him. But he was already sleeping, lying sweetly dead in that clear, limitless water filled with eternal calm. . . .

Milton Keynes UK
Ingram Content Group UK Ltd.
UKHW040739180824
446934UK00013B/125